For Mama Earth and all her creatures.
LD

———

For my grandchildren—Casey, Veronica, Sasha, Marley, Holden, Jasper, Sawyer, Chloe, Hudson, Emma, Eliza, Ever, and Isla—and for Gerry, my companion on all journeys.
HMR

This book was written with generous guidance from NRDC, an international environmental organization that has been safeguarding the planet, its people, its animals, and its natural systems for 50 years. The NRDC does not endorse or support any product or company mentioned in this book.

NRDC

"Do the best you can until you know better. Then when you know better, do better.

—Maya Angelou

Imagine it!

a handbook for a happier planet

Laurie David + Heather Reisman

RODALE

NEW YORK

SUSTAINABLE
FORESTRY
INITIATIVE

Certified Sourcing
www.sfiprogram.org
SFI-01881

The text paper is SFI certified

Published in the United States by Rodale Books, an imprint of Random House,
a division of Penguin Random House LLC, New York.
rodalebooks.com

RODALE and the Plant colophon are registered trademarks
of Penguin Random House LLC.

Originally published in paperback in Canada by Indigo Press, Toronto, in 2020.

Photographs credits appear on page 248.

Library of Congress Cataloging-in-Publication Data is available.

ISBN 978-0-593-23515-7
Ebook ISBN 978-0-593-23516-4

Printed in the United States of America

10 9 8 7 6 5 4 3 2 1

First U.S. Edition

TABLE OF CONTENTS

———

There is now more
in the air than
last 3 million years,
in human

carbon dioxide

at any time in the

which is to say,

history.

PREFACE

We *are* at a defining moment in history.

There has been no bigger shock to our system than the coronavirus pandemic that hit early in 2020 and is still in full force as this book goes to press. It will take years before we fully absorb the impact and lessons of this world-shaking event. But already two things are clear.

One: **We can make bold change.**

In March 2020, and in the blink of an eye, we, for the most part, transformed into people who social-distanced, wore masks, and quickly adapted to working from home. We even stopped hugging our loved ones for the greater good. This is indeed bold change.

Two: **Environmental injustice is raging and cannot be denied.**

When we dug just below the surface of the COVID-19 statistics, we saw that a systemic lack of access to quality health care and far greater exposure to environmental pollutants resulted in people of color dying in far greater numbers than white people. This is wrong and must change.

Let's take the early and important lessons inherent in this moment as inspiration to tackle the climate crisis that is bearing down on us—it is an existential threat like no other.

—

Hi ... I'm Laurie David.

This book has its origins in the many walks I have taken with my dear friend Heather Reisman. Inevitably, the subject of climate would come up; and, in addition to sharing our newest learnings and efforts, I would vent my frustration that the world was not moving fast enough. Her point: lots of people seem to care and want to do more, but often don't know where to start.

That discussion, revisited many times, led to the idea for **Imagine It!** Our objective would be to create an easy-to-digest handbook for anyone who wants to live more sustainably and just needs a bit of help to power the effort.

Although we arrived at the idea to research and write this book together, we approached the task from different perspectives and at different points in our respective eco journeys.

This turned out to be an advantage as we pushed each other to learn more and better explain how our conscious and unconscious habits are contributing to the mess we are in. It forced us to take a hard and honest look at our own fails and wins. And to share, in absorbable fashion, steps for making positive change.

For the record: I was not born an environmentalist.

My journey to take better care of myself and the planet started seriously the moment I became pregnant and realized I would soon be fully responsible for another human being. My initial focus was on food: How was what I was eating going to affect my baby? Did everything have to be organic now? What about the paint for her nursery—might it be toxic? Was the detergent I was using safe for baby clothes, or did it contain harmful chemicals? What would be better for the baby, cloth diapers or disposable? And which option was better for the environment?

I read everything I could get my hands on and soon felt compelled to share what I was learning with other moms. I held discussions at my home and invited experts to share their knowledge.

A big step forward for me was joining the board of NRDC—then called by its full name, the Natural Resources Defense Council.

I will never forget a lunch I had with John Adams, NRDC's founder and one of my environmental heroes. I asked him for advice on how to be most effective as an advocate for the planet. He leaned in and said, "Laurie, you need to focus on only one thing: global warming. Everything you care about will be impacted by that. It is the mother of all issues."

Wow, big lightbulb moment for me.

At that point, I was a stay-at-home mom of two little girls and was lucky to be able to make working on the environment my part-time job. I put all my effort into helping permeate popular culture with issues related to global warming.

In the early 2000s, I authored two books, wrote magazine articles, and produced TV specials on the environment for HBO and Fox News. The culmination of that period was working with former Vice President Al Gore and a great film team to produce what became the Academy Award–winning documentary *An Inconvenient Truth*. More recently I was executive producer of *The Biggest Little Farm*, a film I considered a bookend to *An Inconvenient Truth*, about one family's odyssey to create harmony between nature and themselves.

And my journey continues. Today, together with my husband, I live a good part of my life on a regenerative farm, where we grow a lot of our own food and benefit from a recently installed solar panel tracking system powerful enough to provide clean energy for all our energy needs well into the future.

I am still learning and remain hopeful that we can come together and solve our looming climate crisis. This book is a small contribution to our collective resolve to move boldly toward positive change. I know we can!

Hello ... My name is Heather Reisman.

Laurie David is my dear friend and my partner in documentary filmmaking, including most recently *Fed Up* and *The Social Dilemma*. More relevant to this book, Laurie has been my constant inspiration as I travel this path toward becoming a more environmentally curious and conscious human being.

Like so many of you who will pick up this book, my understanding of what is happening to our planet, and my motivation to take meaningful action, has grown in fits and starts.

Laurie is the one who helped me move from being aware and somewhat interested in discussions on our climate crisis to feeling compelled to make changes in the way I shop, eat, work, and live. I have a way to go to reach my goal of living carbon neutral, but I do more and learn more every day. This book has grown out of my many discussions with Laurie and others; as well as my successful and less successful experiences as I move to replace old habits with new ones that are truly respectful of this place we all call home.

Mostly it exists because I felt everyone would love to have Laurie as a personal "green living" coach; and because we both felt that by combining our different perspectives, we could create a book that would make a difference. Oh, and there is the fact that I love words and books. Which brings me to my day job.

When I am not working on some side-hustle project with Laurie, I am the CEO of Indigo, a Living With Intention Company that began its life as a bookseller and still has books and ideas at its core. At Indigo, we are just beginning our eco journey, but we are totally committed to becoming a net zero company in as short a time as possible.

Finally, as the mother of four and the grandmother of thirteen, I have every reason to put my heart and soul into doing whatever I can to make things better for the future.

From Both of Us:

One of us is American (LD), one of us is Canadian (HMR). In writing this, we have done our best to bring in narratives from both countries while recognizing that many of the issues are universal and data from one country is likely to be closely linked to data and experience from another. Hopefully, we have struck a good balance; that has been our intent throughout. What we believe for sure is that, ultimately, it is one world.

Happy reading. ☺

ABOUT THIS BOOK

———

Welcome to **Imagine It!**—a handbook for anyone wanting to begin or advance a journey toward living in better balance with our planet. This book is meant to inspire you, support you, and make it easy for you to replace old, planet-hurting habits with new and healthy ones—that is to say, to make your personal contribution to reversing our global warming crisis and enhancing your own health and well-being.

Assertion: Not a single person who picks up this book intentionally decided to live in a manner that contributes to environmental degradation and global warming.

Reality: Our harmful impact on the planet happened as we became more and more dependent on fossil fuels and embraced all that modern-day life had to offer. Without conscious intention but having grown up with all that the 20th century brought to us, we have become people who buy, use, and do things that are wasteful and damaging to our environment and often to our own health.

Making matters worse and unjust, for decades BIPOC (Black, Indigenous, People of Color) communities the world over have disproportionately shouldered the repercussions of our fossil fuel–based lifestyle and the resulting climate change.

It is now time, in fact past time, that we fully and boldly engage, and course correct.

This book is one small contribution to shifting our understanding and behaviors. It is about developing new mindsets and then making personal and collective change that will lead to a healthier planet and a healthier us.

In these pages, we highlight the need to change some of our food, clothing, and transportation habits, and meaningfully lower our use of plastic, paper, water, and harmful chemicals.

We call the changes in these areas **lifestyle shifts**; and there is a chapter devoted to each one of them. Each chapter begins with a short story on the shift being explored, and then provides clear steps for replacing old habits with new ones.

We know—it sounds like a lot. But keep reading. It is easier than you might think. And we know from experience that taking planet-positive actions is hugely satisfying.

This book also highlights the role each person can play to influence necessary changes in business practices and, perhaps more important, in government regulation. We as consumers and citizens have so much power to effect change. Our voices on social media can create multiplier effect momentum. Manufacturers and retailers, as well as those hoping to be elected to office, are keenly connected to what we are saying, what we are doing, and how we spend our hard-earned dollars. Many people making individual changes ultimately leads to a collective will and inevitably business and government action. And this is exactly what we need!

Underpinning everything in this book are these beliefs:

Being an environmentalist is as basic as wanting to drink clean water and breathe clean air.

Becoming an environmentally thoughtful and engaged person is a journey. It is about growing more aware of our various "footprints" and then, at as significant a pace as possible, taking steps to reduce those footprints. The key is to learn, act, and stay on the journey.

Being an environmentalist is not about being "perfect" all the time, because no one ever is. It's about being open to a learning curve and making determined progress.

Making small everyday changes helps develop our overall mindset and ultimately results in shifting our attitudes on the big issues, i.e., who we vote for and what we expect of our companies and our representatives.

Our votes matter. We need to use our voices and our votes to elect leaders who are fully committed to implementing regulations to reverse global warming.

IMAGINE IT!

———

You needn't read **Imagine It!** in order, from beginning to end. You can pick a chapter of interest to you and just dive in. You can read this introduction and move right to the chapter on Clothing and then return to an earlier one. Whatever feels right for you.

If you simply do one chapter a month, you will wake up in a few months and discover you have made amazing progress as an environmentalist. Suggestion: if you have kids, involve them in all you are learning and doing.

As we noted earlier—each chapter begins with a very short "story" on the footprint being explored. We mean for these short stories to give you some important context about the problem being explored. But in every case there is so much more that can be learned if you are interested. For this reason, we have included a list of books and websites in the Appendix that will allow you to delve more deeply.

Sprinkled throughout are some pages marked **NOTES**. We are all for writing in the book as ideas come to mind, whether using these specially marked pages or any of the margins. You might even find it fun to keep track of the changes you are implementing.

Also note that there is a glossary at the back of the book, which will help if you come across a term or an acronym with which you may not be familiar.

Things to keep in mind while reading:

- Environmental health and personal health are intricately connected. We are in constant interaction with our environment—breathing the air, drinking the water, and eating the food that comes from the land, oceans, rivers, and streams which surround us. As goes the health of all of these, so goes our own health.

- Our planet, like our bodies, is a system. Everything is interconnected. Environmental damage in one area will very likely set off a chain reaction of damaging effects in other areas.

- Conversely, taking action to replace harmful activity will most likely result in positive impacts elsewhere in our ecosystem. The more we understand these connections, the more we will make good choices. So...

Let's get started.

"How you imagine the world determines how you live in it."

—David Suzuki

Scientist, author, broadcaster, climate activist

Imagine a world where clean, green, and healthy are our default settings.

Imagine a global culture that nurtures respect for our limited resources and rejects dependence on fossil fuels.

Imagine a world in which we live in balance with our life-sustaining forests, grasslands, and wetlands.

Imagine a world where regenerative farms are the norm and most of our food is organic, affordable, and available to everyone.

Imagine a world where our oceans are healthy and our corals and marine life breathe with ease.

Imagine a world where clean drinking water is abundant and available for all.

Imagine a collective outcry so bold, so determined, and so sustained that governments and businesses have no choice but to take real action to reverse our climate crisis.

Close your eyes and imagine it.

Keep imagining ...

Now, let's do it.
Let's make the
shift to what we
just envisioned.

Our Plastic Footprint

There is no such thing as 'away.' When we throw anything away, it must go somewhere.

—Annie Leonard, *The Story of Stuff*

FACT: We produce more than 380 million tons of plastic waste worldwide every year.

FACT: On our current trajectory, one report estimates that in 50 years plastic will outweigh the fish in our oceans.

FACT: One million plastic water bottles are purchased every minute around the world; approximately 1.1 billion toothbrushes are tossed every year in North America.

FACT: We ingest about 2,000 microplastic particles a week. That is the equivalent of a credit card of plastic every seven days.

FACT: The US uses more than 36 billion disposable utensils a year. Laid end to end they would wrap around the globe 139 times.

The Short Story on Plastic

There is a very direct connection between plastic and global warming. And the connection is this: Most plastic is made from fossil fuels—oil, natural gas, coal. The process of extracting and transporting those fossil fuels, and then manufacturing and distributing the plastic products, creates millions of tons of greenhouse gases annually.

Then, at the end of its life cycle, plastic further damages our environment when it ends up in landfills or becomes litter in our oceans.

Plastic waste in landfills can end up leaching toxic chemicals into nearby soil and into the groundwater that supports local drinking water systems. Keep in mind, many of these landfills are in our own communities—and disproportionately where poor people and people of color live.

Plastic in the ocean often breaks down into tiny bits and pieces called microplastics, which may get swallowed by fish that mistake them for food. Eventually, some of these micro amounts may get swallowed by us when we eat tuna, salmon, or sushi. Microplastics have even ended up in breast milk.

Let's dig a bit deeper.

Because plastic is inexpensive, we have come to use it for lots of products that are created for single or short-term use. Think plastic water bottles, disposable razors, our daily personal care products, and all those cheap pens and cigarette lighters that are forever getting lost.

When we toss all this disposable plastic, we create a huge environmental mess because plastic never fully biodegrades. Every single bit of plastic any of us has ever touched—the wrap on the salad, the polystyrene cup at soccer practice, the red Solo cup at that party, every toothbrush used since childhood, every Ziploc bag holding a peanut butter sandwich, the lid on every cup of coffee, the dental floss you use every night—it's all still lingering somewhere on our planet.

Unless we take action, on our current trajectory, the problem is about to get worse. A lot worse. Why? Because as renewable

Environmental Injustice

Recently (2020) the oil and gas industry has been lobbying US trade officials to strike a deal with Kenya, part of which would encourage them to accept our discarded plastic waste and play a role encouraging other African nations to do the same. In other words—let's take our pollution and send it elsewhere. This is the very opposite of environmental justice.

energy moves to replace oil and gas, the fossil fuel industry is scrambling for new uses for its plastic by-products. And there is a big market for single and short-term-use consumer products.

Whales Need Our Love

In a heartbreaking news story, we learned that a sperm whale washed ashore in Scotland with more than 200 pounds of plastic in its gut.

Busting the recycling myth: We have all been taught to believe that if we put our plastic waste in a recycle bin, it will be recycled and then reused. Alas, this is simply not the case.

The whole concept of plastic recycling was promoted as a solution to plastic waste. But it's hugely misleading. The fact is, only 9 percent of all plastic ever gets recycled. The other 91 percent ends up in our oceans, on our beaches, and in landfills where it causes real harm. Even the 9 percent is at some risk given that it is now often cheaper to buy new plastic rather than recycled material—so demand for it could go down.

All this to say, recycling has benefits but it is for sure not the answer to our plastic pollution problem.

Key Takeaway:

We are using far too much disposable plastic, which ends up as trash—and this trash is trashing our world. We need to stop buying it, tossing it, and using so much of it. We need to move to a world in which far less new plastic is created and existing plastic gets reclaimed, recycled, and reused.

Notes:

-
-
-
-

Develop an "allergy" to plastic.

This shift is about building our awareness of the amount of disposable plastic we use daily; and then developing new habits that meaningfully cut down the amount of plastic in our life.

Step 1: Build your awareness

Take a clear-eyed look at the plastic you use every day.

Plastic at home

- Call a family meeting to discuss your plastic habits (or call yourself to a meeting to have this talk).

- Make a list of all the disposable plastic items that you and your family use. If you live with others, and especially if you have kids, it's fun to turn this into a family challenge to see whose list is the shortest and whose list needs the most work.

- Once you have your first draft, double-check it by taking a trip around your house to see what you might have missed. Check out the kitchen, the bedroom, the bathroom, the closets, the basement, and where you do laundry. Don't forget to look under your sink and inside your shower.

- Check out your refrigerator and pantry to assess the number of items you are buying that are in plastic packages or containers. Then check the bottom of the containers. Most plastic containers have a small number inside the three-arrow-triangle recycling symbol. The numbers are a way of classifying whether the container is recyclable. If the containers have a low number on the bottom—1 or 2—they are likely recyclable. Any number above this cannot be recycled.

Plastic when shopping or eating out

- Mentally go through your day. Did your smoothie come in a plastic cup? Did your lunch come with plastic utensils? Did your salad come in a plastic clamshell?

- Actively pay attention to the plastic packaging and pouches that are part of the purchases you make, including at the grocery. (Keep this in mind for purchases made through e-shopping as well.) How is the product itself packaged by the manufacturer, and then how is it further packaged for you by the retailer? This consciousness will begin to permeate your thinking and then just naturally guide your choices and your advocacy.

- Consolidate your notes into a full list to get a clear picture of the disposable plastic in your life.

I Can See Clearly Now

Ali Rose VanOverbeke launched Genusee to give a second life to the many disposable plastic water bottles that have been used by residents of Flint, Michigan, to address lead poisoning in their water system. Genusee manufactures upcycled sunglasses and reading glasses right in Flint. Each pair upcycles 15 discarded water bottles.

Says VanOverbeke—"The future has to become circular or we won't have a planet."

Step 2: Take action

Fall in love with reusable water bottles and mugs.

- Stop paying for bottled water. If you haven't already, buy a reusable water bottle or two for use at the office, when you are out shopping, going to the gym, or traveling. Glass, aluminum, or steel are best. NOTE: Be sure the bottle you choose is marked BPA (Bisphenol A) free.

- Make this a family affair by including your kids in this practice. Start them off young with good habits and avoid their becoming used to disposable plastic bottles.

- Caffeinating on the go? Carry your coffee in a travel mug whenever you can. At some coffee retailers, you'll even be rewarded with a discount when you bring your own container.

- Share the love. There are so many beautifully designed and sustainably made water bottles and coffee thermos mugs. Consider these as great host, birthday, or holiday gifts.

Grocery shop with reusable bags

- Carry reusable shopping bags and reusable produce and food bags. Eliminating the plastic bags for produce and the clam shells on prewashed greens would be a great step.

- Keep reusable shopping bags in your car and return them to the trunk as soon as they are emptied.

- Ditto reusable produce/food bags for fruits, vegetables, and bulk items such as nuts, dried fruits, rice, grains, dried beans, etc.

- Tuck a few shopping bags into your favorite backpack or piece of luggage so you have one handy if you are traveling.

- If you go to the local market on the weekend, have fun with a large market basket. They are now easy to find and affordable.

Bag your dry cleaning

- Bring your own garment bag to the dry cleaner to pick up and protect your clothing. The amount of plastic and paper waste that can be saved is meaningful. (**NOTE**: We revisit dry cleaning as it relates to the chemicals used in a later chapter.)

Reduce plastic in the kitchen, laundry area, and bathroom

- Stock up on reusable containers, lids, mason jars, and beeswax wrap to replace plastic wrap in the fridge or pantry.

- Avoid buying paper cups or polystyrene—better known to most of us as Styrofoam cups. Polystyrene foam is particularly bad for the environment and for us humans. It contains styrene, which is classified as carcinogenic.

- Say goodbye to plastic sandwich bags and plastic wrap. There are many great alternatives for school lunch or when you bring lunch to work. We love bento boxes, picnic tins, cloth sandwich bags, silicone sleeves, and beeswax covers. If you do occasionally use plastic bags for food, do rinse and reuse.

- Carry a little roll-up pack of utensils, including a reusable, non-plastic straw. Keep them in your bag so you can say no to disposable plastic forks and spoons. This will start putting a dent in the 100 million plastic utensils that are used and thrown away in the US alone each day!

- Choose laundry detergent and cleaning products that are packaged in environmentally friendly packaging—whether refillable or recyclable. If you're choosing capsules, look for a brand that does not wrap the capsule in plastic because the plastic melts and ends up going down the drain and into the water system.

- Replace plastic bags used in the kitchen, whether for food or for garbage, with alternatives that are equally effective and compostable. There are many on the market to choose from.

- Buy sponges made from earth-friendly materials, like plants, cellulose, or walnut shells. Most sponges are made from plastic and shed micro plastic particles that go down the drain.

- Replace disposable razors with steel, reusable, or eco-friendly options.

- Switch to a toothbrush made with an environmentally friendly material or one where you just change the bristles when required.

- Try a shampoo and conditioner in bar form. Again, there are many great choices on the market. Bar soap and conditioner go directly to shifting our lifelong habit of using liquid shampoo/conditioner from a plastic bottle. (LD: At first, I was skeptical that the bar of conditioner could deal with

Doing Well and Doing Good

Two friends on a trip to Thailand were appalled at the amount of plastic trash in the country's beautiful waters. Angry but inspired, they came back with an idea that became By Humankind, a company now creating beautiful personal care products that come in bar form and without any plastic packaging.

Liquid soap in plastic bottles is a big plastic mess.

It was entrepreneur Robert Taylor who first thought to liquefy soap and package it in a plastic bottle. This was back in 1978. He was inspired to invent this when he noticed the mess left on a soap dish after he washed his hands. His first product, Softsoap, was a smash success and set in motion what is now a multibillion-dollar plastic-bottle liquid soap industry. Mr. Taylor likely never imagined that by fixing a little mess, he would create a much bigger one. Nearly 500 billion plastic bottles are produced every year worldwide.

my curly, unruly hair, but it worked great!)

- Treat yourself to something fun with all the money you save switching to a reusable lifestyle.

- Though not plastic, we can't help but mention, aluminum foil wrap is also very harmful to the environment and pollutes at every stage of its life.

Leave the glitter on the retailers' shelves

- Do your best to avoid buying products with glitter, whether it's greeting cards or makeup, children's clothing or arts and crafts products. This falls under the "Who Knew?" category. It turns out our attraction to glitter is causing problems for the environment. Glitter is made from plastic and contributes to the microplastic buildup in our oceans. It has also been found to break down and release chemicals harmful to human and animal health.

- Say no to balloons. The worst are those that are filled with helium, as they often escape into the air and become litter that is dangerous to birds and sea life. It is estimated that over 100,000 marine mammals die each year from balloon entanglement or ingestion.

Become an advocate

Write to the CEOs of your favorite brands to let them know about the changes you would like to see in their products or packaging. Let them know that your continued support depends on their having a time-based plan to become good environmental stewards.

Reach out to your local, state/province, and federal representatives and advocate for legislation that meaningfully lessens plastic pollution.

Start or support a local plastic-bag ban if this is not already the law in your city.

Consider supporting an organization fighting pollution, whether the problem is in your neighborhood or someone else's neighborhood. One inspiring example is Rise St. James. This group, started by a fed-up mom, is working to stop Formosa Plastics from building one of the largest factories in the world in their backyard. The planned factory would turn fracked gas into plastic pellets, potentially doubling the toxic air pollution in this largely Black community. The more support they have, the more likely it is they will succeed. David really can beat Goliath with a big enough slingshot. Visit www.uumfe.org, search Rise St. James to learn about this initiative.

To learn about more ways to fight plastic pollution, visit www.plasticpollutioncoalition.org, www.5gyres.org, www.algalita.org, and www.theoceancleanup.org.

Notes:

-
-
-
-
-

It's Time to Break Free From Plastic

Break Free From Plastic is a global movement advocating for a future free from plastic. In 2019, they surveyed 51 countries and 6 continents, sending out volunteers to pick up plastic trash left on beaches, along city streets, and in streams and rivers. Of the plastic they collected, products from Coca-Cola created the most plastic debris, with Nestlé and PepsiCo products close behind.

Until now, Coca-Cola, Nestlé, and PepsiCo have fought against any plastic bottle ban, bottle tax, or return policies. Yet these are the very legislative policies that would force them to embrace recycling and/or innovate away from their use of plastic altogether. Become an advocate: write and encourage the CEOs of these companies to take positive steps to eliminate plastic waste.

www.breakfreefromplastic.org

Our Food Footprint

Treasure the farmer, nurture the soil, learn from nature, eat whole food, and share the harvest.

—Alice Waters

FACT: Conventional food production is responsible for one-quarter of the world's greenhouse gas emissions.

FACT: Consumers are responsible for more wasted food than farmers, grocery stores, or any other part of the food supply chain. The average household of four is throwing away approximately $1,800 of food a year.

FACT: A conventionally grown apple orchard may be sprayed up to 16 times a year with more than 30 different chemicals.

FACT: Most antibiotics sold in the US are given to livestock— not humans.

A Short Story on Food

Food—we love it. We need it. But if we want enough good food to feed us all, and if we want a healthy planet, we need to make changes in how we produce food, what food we consume, and how much food we waste. (Food insecurity and lack of access to healthy food for the marginalized and disadvantaged throughout the world, including the US and Canada, is a critical subject, for a whole other book.)

Let's dig in ...

On food production

We used to grow and raise our food the right way—on small to medium-sized farms, with a small number of animals, producing a wide variety of crops that were rotated regularly to protect the richness of the soil. Over time, our population exploded, we began eating larger portions, often including meat at every meal, and our food tastes changed. Think cheeseburgers, hot dogs, fried chicken, steak, pizza, breakfast sausage, mac and cheese.

These changes, coupled with technology advances, have helped push farming into an industrialized model that has significant negative impact on our ecosystem.

On meat and dairy

Today, in many parts of North America, large numbers of beef and dairy cattle, pigs, and chickens are grown in big industrial operations. At every step in the farming process—from growing the animal feed (corn and soy), to raising and slaughtering the animals, to processing and distributing the end food products—significant greenhouse gases are released. Included in this buildup of global-warming gases is climate-polluting methane produced by the animals themselves when they digest the feed and defecate.

What's the Beef with Beef?

A 2017 NRDC report found that beef from industrially raised cattle has the highest carbon footprint of any food and contributes 34 percent of total diet-related climate-warming pollution.

In addition to the carbon pollution issue, the industrial meat farming industry creates other environmental stresses. The industry is a huge user of water, is responsible for significant amounts of water pollution, and contributes to soil degradation through monoculture farming. The industry also uses our precious antibiotics, weakening their effectiveness when we need them for our kids and ourselves.

A note on this last point about antibiotics, as the connection between antibiotic use in animals and our own antibiotic use is not obvious: Antibiotics are infused into the diet of many animals—especially cattle and pigs—to prevent illnesses they *might* get due to the cramped and unsanitary conditions in which they are kept. The more antibiotics are used in industrial farming, the more resistant the superbugs become, and the less effective those drugs are for us. Not good.

About fruits and vegetables

There is also an issue with conventionally farmed fruits and vegetables. Environmentally harmful chemicals are used liberally to supersize crops, kill weeds, and destroy pests. These chemicals degrade the soil, run off into our waterways, and even kill bees—the crucial pollinators we need to fertilize our crops. FYI: Bees are responsible for one out of every three bites of food we eat! We badly need these insanely hard workers.

A word on fish

While there are some issues with industrial fish farming, the bigger problem is in our oceans, which are becoming increasingly less hospitable to marine life. Fish are suffering and dying from rising ocean temperatures, overfishing, man-made ocean noise, massive plastic debris, and increased levels of mercury and acidification. In the short term, this means we will have to be very careful about which and how much fish we eat. For the long term, to protect our vital marine life, we need to get serious now about reversing the trends that threaten it.

The food we toss

Food waste also packs an environmental punch. When we throw away limp lettuce, wobbly carrots, bruised tomatoes, or leftovers that no longer look appetizing, we rarely think about the impact of our actions on the climate.

Food thrown into the garbage ends up decomposing in landfills, usually somewhere near your town or city, where it releases significant and harmful greenhouse gases. Let's not forget about the cost of the water, carbon emissions, and labor used in growing the uneaten food in the first place.

Key Takeaway:

The food habits we have developed over time are proving to be too demanding on our planet. We need to buy, store, eat, and discard food with deliberate thought. Mother Earth is here for us, we need to be here for her.

Reduce your food footprint.

This shift is about becoming more thoughtful about the foods we choose, being intentional about what we really need and want to eat, and throwing away far less. The planet, our bodies, and our wallets will be grateful for the changes we make.

Step 1: Build your awareness

- Do the one-week food test. For seven days, keep track of what you and your family eat, as well as how much you throw out at the end of a meal. Take note if you are also tossing things from the fridge at the end of the week.

- If you are inspired, track how much of your diet is the most demanding on the planet. See chart below.

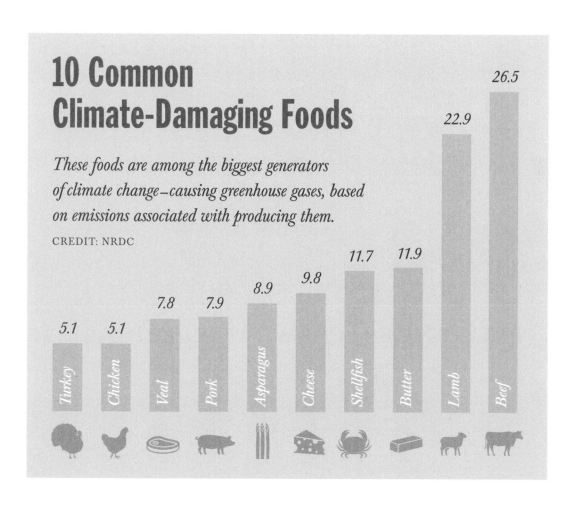

10 Common Climate-Damaging Foods

These foods are among the biggest generators of climate change–causing greenhouse gases, based on emissions associated with producing them.

CREDIT: NRDC

Turkey	Chicken	Veal	Pork	Asparagus	Cheese	Shellfish	Butter	Lamb	Beef
5.1	5.1	7.8	7.9	8.9	9.8	11.7	11.9	22.9	26.5

Step 2: Take action

Choose your foods with the planet and your health in mind.

Eat less meat

- Consider shifting plant-based food and grains to the center of the plate and reducing the amount of meat and dairy you consume. In addition to being better for the planet, studies show that eating less meat reduces the risk of heart disease, stroke, diabetes, cancer, and obesity.

- Join the Meatless Monday movement, or pick any day to skip eating meat.

Interesting fact: If everyone in the world ate just one less hamburger a week, it would take the equivalent of 10 million cars off the road every year.
CREDIT: NRDC

- Become a weekday vegetarian and enjoy meat on the weekend—or do the reverse.

- Check out the many options for plant-based meat substitutes that are growing in popularity, such as Impossible Burger, Beyond Meat, and Gardein.

Consume less dairy

It might surprise you to know that cheese and butter are two of the most greenhouse gas–intensive foods you can add to your shopping cart. According to NRDC, butter is the third most climate-damaging food, because it takes 21 pounds of milk to produce just one pound of butter.

- Try to cut back on your dairy intake.

- Consider buying plant-based milks. Soymilk, rice milk, oat milk, almond milk, cashew milk, coconut milk, and hemp milk are delicious options. Almost all alternative milks have lower greenhouse gas footprints than milk from cows.

A Word about Oat Milk

Looking for an eco alternative to milk? Look no further than oat milk, which has exploded in popularity over the last few years. It has a creamy consistency close to milk, and is one of the most environmentally friendly choices available because oats themselves require less water and land and produce less greenhouse gases than almond or cow milk.

- When consuming cheeses, lean toward softer ones, which leave lower footprints because they contain less milk solids.

- Go easy on the Greek yogurt! It and other kinds of strained yogurt take four times as much milk to make as regular yogurt.

If buying meat, and if at all possible, buy organic, antibiotic-free meat

- Organically grown foods are farmed without the use of chemical pesticides, yielding benefits for both our health and our soil. Organic means less pesticide and synthetic fertilizer use. Farming organically also builds soil health and mitigates climate change.

- If you can afford it, buy organically grown, antibiotic-free meat. One of the benefits of buying less meat, which is generally an expensive item in your shopping basket, is that there'll be a little money left over to purchase the good stuff.

Go organic for fruits and vegetables

- Whenever possible, buy organic fruits and vegetables to limit your exposure to pesticides. For example, glyphosate, the active ingredient in the pesticide Roundup, is commonly sprayed in conventional fruit and vegetable farming. Glyphosate has been linked to cancer.

PASTURE
RAISED
NO HORMONES
GRASS
FED
NO ANTIBIOTICS
NO
GMOS

MELOGOLD
GRAPEFRUIT
$3.00
PER POUND

CHERIMOYA
$12.00
PER POUND

RA CARA
RANGES
$6.00
PER POUND

OCADOS
5.00
POUND

OROBLANCO
GRAPEFRUIT
$3.00/LB

- If you can't buy all organic, try for it when buying the produce that the Environmental Working Group (EWG) has labeled "the Dirty Dozen," so called because, when grown conventionally, they have the most pesticide residue. The Dirty Dozen are: kale, strawberries, spinach, nectarines, peaches, tomatoes, apples, grapes, pears, cherries, celery, and potatoes.

Interesting fact: A recent study by internationally respected Friends of the Earth showed that an organic diet lowered the levels of the toxic chemical glyphosate in children and adults.

Buy local
Buy in season

- Buying local and in season has many benefits. In addition to lowering carbon emissions from trucking, you are supporting local growers and getting to enjoy food at its freshest and tastiest.

Be thoughtful about which fish you eat and how often you eat it

Think small. The lower the fish is on the food chain, the less mercury it contains. Mercury is especially dangerous for pregnant or nursing women and young children.

NOTE: Mercury is spewed into the air from coal-burning power plants and factories. Once in the air, it drifts down into lakes, rivers, and oceans, where it is eventually absorbed or ingested by fish. Big predatory fish, like sharks or tuna, can have especially high concentrations of mercury in their bodies.

When dining out, choose fish with the planet in mind

- Consult www.seafoodwatch.org to get clear information on the healthiest and most sustainable fish to buy at the store or eat when you are at a restaurant. Seafood Watch uses a rigorous, science-based process to categorize seafood as "best choices," "good alternatives," or "avoid." The "avoid" category includes fish that are overfished or caught/farmed in ways that harm other marine life or the environment.

- When out to dinner and ordering fish, ask your server or, if you can, the chef if the fish is local or imported. Increasingly, imported seafood is raised in factory-farm conditions in which the fish are exposed to dangerous antibiotics and chemicals. Asking these questions shows the restaurant that you care. Your server may not always know the answer, but if we all continue to ask the question, we will help raise awareness and spur positive change.

- If possible, order wild or locally caught fish.

Mercury in Fish

Least Mercury

Anchovies	Herring	Sardine
Butterfish	Mackerel	Scallop*
Catfish	(N. Atlantic, Chub)	Shad (American)
Clam	Mullet	Shrimp*
Crab (Domestic)	Oyster	Sole (Pacific)
Crawfish/Crayfish	Perch (Ocean)	Squid (Calamari)
Croaker (Atlantic)	Plaice	Tilapia
Flounder*	Pollock	Trout (Freshwater)
Haddock (Atlantic)*	Salmon (Canned)**	Whitefish
Hake	Salmon (Fresh)**	Whiting

Moderate Mercury

Eat six servings or less per month:

Bass (Striped, Black)	Jacksmelt (Silverside)	Skate*
Carp	Lobster	Snapper*
Cod (Alaskan)	Mahi Mahi	Tuna (Canned
Croaker (White Pacific)	Monkfish*	chunk light)
Halibut (Atlantic)*	Perch (Freshwater)	Tuna (Skipjack)*
Halibut (Pacific)	Sablefish	Weakfish (Sea Trout)

High Mercury

Eat three servings or less per month:

Bluefish   Mackerel   Tuna
Grouper*   (Spanish, Gulf)   (Canned Albacore)
                Sea Bass (Chilean)* Tuna (Yellowfin)*

Highest Mercury

Avoid eating:

Mackerel (King)   Shark*   Tuna (Bigeye, Ahi)*
Marlin*   Swordfish*
Orange Roughy*   Tilefish*

---

*Fish in Trouble! These fish are perilously low in numbers or are caught using environmentally destructive methods. **Farmed salmon may contain PCBs, chemicals with serious long-term health effects.*

Information in this guide is based on averages from the FDA's test results for mercury in fish and the EPA's determination of safe levels of mercury for women of reproductive age. Some individual fish have mercury concentrations significantly higher than the average. For more details, see: www.nrdc.org/mercury.

Avoid palm oil

It turns out not all oils are created equal. Palm oil, which is a major driver of deforestation, pollution, and habitat loss for endangered species (think orangutans, rhinos, and tigers), is still being used for cooking and as an ingredient in so many food products. In fact, palm oil is found in a shocking number of things we all love—from pizza to margarine, from peanut butter to cookies and chocolate.

Beware: Palm oil may be an ingredient in your food without you even knowing because it goes by many names, including vegetable fat, palm kernel, palm kernel oil, palm fruit oil, vegetable oil, palmate, palmitate, palmolein, glyceryl, stearate, stearic acid, elaeis guineensis, palmitic acid, palm stearine, palmitoyl oxostearamide, palmitoyl tetrapeptide-3, sodium laureth sulfate, sodium lauryl sulfate, sodium kernelate, isopropylmyristate. (HMR/LD: Wow ... hard to keep track of all these names!)

- Read labels and stop buying products with palm oil.

- Let the general manager of your favorite grocery store know why you aren't buying products with palm oil. They have the power to become great advocates for formulation change.

- If you have time, write a letter to food manufacturers that use palm oil and express your deep concern about its use.

Cut down on your food waste

Try to plan as many meals as you can a few days ahead of time, including any meals taken to school or work.

- Take the time to plan meals. Planning meals relieves stress and keeps you from buying food you may not use. Added benefits of meal planning: you will eat healthier and throw away less. It also helps you avoid the last-minute "what to make for dinner" dilemma that often ends up in a paper-boxed pizza or fast-food takeout—including all of the disposables that come with it.

- Develop a love affair with your freezer, knowing the only thing fresher than fresh is frozen fresh.

The Uglier the Better

Thousands of truckloads of misshapen but otherwise perfectly good fruit is thrown away every year. One smart and caring family of farmers in California had a very good idea: they looked at this terrible food waste problem and saw it as an opportunity. So was born The Ugly Company. Ugly upcycles rejected fruit—as in fruit with little bumps, scratches, or nicks—and turns it into delicious dried fruit snacks. Every package prevents at least two pounds of perfectly healthy but ugly fruit from becoming waste. Their motto says it all: beautiful on the inside!

- Keep a stock of environmentally friendly reusable containers of various sizes for easy freezing. Quickly freezing leftovers is a fantastic way to avoid waste and save money.

- Remember to freeze leftovers into dinner-sized portions that work for you and can be easily defrosted when you need them.

Interesting fact: The two biggest causes of food waste in the home are leftovers that are thrown away and fresh produce that spoils because it has not been used.

- Make soup. It's easy. At the end of the week, instead of throwing away the fading veggies, toss them into a soup. Boil whatever you have on hand in salted water along with some sautéed chopped onion and garlic and you have a great, healthy meal.

- Keep masking tape and a Sharpie close by to label and date everything you freeze.

Take expiration dates with a grain of salt

- Of course, you should never eat or drink bad food, but smell a product before throwing it out. Dates on food packages are usually approximate indications of when the food might be at its best, not absolute confirmation of when something has gone bad. For most foods, these dates are not regulated by the federal government and can be arbitrary.

Store your fresh herbs in a glass with water

- This idea does double duty. You can use the herbs as a centerpiece for your table and then store them overnight either in the fridge or on your counter. (LD/HMR: We are both doing this and having a "raging" debate. LD says fridge is better. HMR is having more luck on the counter.)
  In any case, you will be pleasantly surprised at how much longer your herbs last when treated to this hydrating approach. Stored this way, herbs can last two weeks.

- And, speaking of herbs, it is fun growing small pots of your favorites on your kitchen windowsill. Pick as needed, savor the taste, and congratulate yourself on avoiding the more expensive, plastic-packaged, less tasty versions found at the grocery store.

Ease up on perfection

- Often food is thrown away simply because of aesthetics: it's not red enough, it has a bump, it's a little misshapen. Fruits and vegetables rejected by shoppers more than likely end up in that landfill we talked about. Let's embrace small imperfections. By the way ... this may be a good metaphor for other aspects of life.

Organize your fridge

A lot of food goes to waste simply because we forget it is there.

- Have a "Marie Kondo" fridge moment (she of the "tidy-up" movement). It can be hugely satisfying to treat your fridge to the same burst of organization that Ms. Kondo recommends we bestow on our cupboards from time to time. Take everything out and then reorganize—and enjoy the results.

- When loading the fridge, keep food that needs to be eaten first toward the front and place newer items behind.

- Different sections of the fridge have different temperatures, so load it up accordingly. Raw meat should always go at the bottom, where it is coldest, and milk should be kept in the body of the fridge, not in the door (which is the warmest), to keep it fresh longest.

- Store food in glass containers, which will help you easily see what you have. This has the added benefit of making everything look so inviting.

- Consider using a lazy Susan or two in your fridge. It makes it super easy to see and access items, and it looks great.

- For more pointers on how to reduce food waste in your home, including recipes and storage tips, check out www.savethefood.com.

Be a composter

- How you throw away your food waste matters. If it's tossed in the garbage, it will ending up rotting in a landfill, where it will release methane, a stronger greenhouse gas than CO_2. If you compost it, you will create biodegradable matter that can be used as fertilizer in your garden, on your trees, or for any pots that you are nurturing. Composting is a feel-good activity.

- Collect daily food scraps such as banana peels, apple cores, ends of veggies, fruit rinds, eggshells, coffee grinds, carrot tops, and even tea bags in a bowl or bucket by the sink.

- Check out city programs; your city may have a compost pickup plan.

- Certain foods don't even need full composting. Eggshells and coffee grounds can easily be crushed up and placed under any tree or bush. Roses love them!

- Google *composting* to learn more about the many options and advantages of composting.

Start a garden

- You don't need a large backyard to plant a garden; any small space you can reclaim will do. Check out a windowsill, your rooftop or balcony, an empty lot in your neighborhood, your kids' schoolyard, even some space alongside your driveway or front curb. Community gardens are becoming more popular. Consider starting one in your neighborhood.

- As a start, lettuce, kale, collards, and tomatoes can easily grow in small spaces. Herbs can grow almost anywhere in small pots.

- Remember: go chemical-free when fertilizing or treating your garden for weeds and other pests.

Protect our bees

As noted earlier, bees pollinate one in every three bites of food we eat. Sadly, our life-sustaining bees are dying in record numbers because of climate change, pesticide use, and loss of habitat. As individuals, we can do a lot to help save these mighty creatures.

- When you can, buy organic fruits and vegetables rather than those that are conventionally grown using bee-harming pesticides and toxic synthetic fertilizers.

- Go pesticide-free at home. We said it before, but we are saying it again: Roundup should be the first product to go! There is growing evidence that its active ingredient, glyphosate, is dangerous to bees as well as to human health.

- If you have a little, or even a larger, garden space, consider planting flowers that bloom at different times to provide a food source for bees over the entire growing season. They particularly like blue, purple, white, and yellow flowers—or so the experts say.

- Bees will love it if you put out water for them. A shallow bowl filled with a few stones makes it easy for the bees to land and take a sip.

- Buy local honey when available. Support your local beekeepers!

Become an advocate

Keep our food clean. Petition your elected officials to ban glyphosate and other toxic chemicals from use in industrial farming. (See draft letter in Appendix ... to use with your local officials.)

Go to nrdc.org/savetheantibiotics and sign the petition encouraging lawmakers to stop the overuse of antibiotics in farming.

If your community does not yet have a commitment to composting, encourage your local officials to start a curbside composting program.

Bees beautiful bees

By Reese Halter, PhD

Bees are incomparable living beings.

Honeybees are the Einsteins of the 900,000-plus insects on our planet. Like us, they are top-down learners, live in a democracy, and are able to recognize an individual human face. They can count, be trained to arrive at specific time intervals, and have a sophisticated dance language. They learn while they are asleep, and they may even dream. Honeybee neurons—those specialized brain cells that transfer information to nerve cells—are strikingly like ours.

Honeybees have long been inspiring my medical colleagues to create innovative remedies. For example, honeybees produce a chemical that they use to stun predators who enter their colonies. It turns out that those "stun chemicals" may have an important role in human medicine as an effective anesthetic.

Other powerful medicines are derived from a glue that honeybees make for their hives. This pungent bee glue called propolis is well endowed with antiviral, antifungal, anti-inflammatory, antibacterial, and cancer-fighting compounds.

Honeybees pollinate one out of every three bites of food we eat. We need them!

Sadly, since 2005, hundreds of billions of American honeybees have died horribly. The climate crisis and the nerve poisons in insecticides, along with additional environmental hazards, have coalesced into the perfect deadly storm. It is the nerve poisons in insecticides that rank above all factors in driving the death of honeybees. These insecticides (neonicotinoids, sulfoxaflors, flupyradifurone, and chlorpyrifos) are as much as 10,000 times more toxic than DDT. (DDT has been banned since 1972 in both Canada and the United States for endangering bird species to the point of extinction and as a human cancer-causing agent.) When bees come into contact with these chemicals, they literally lose their minds and shake to death. It's comparable to a healthy human all of a sudden contracting full-strength Alzheimer's and Parkinson's simultaneously.

It's time to get serious about protecting our bees.

Our Clothing Footprint

The most environmentally friendly product is the one you didn't buy.

—Joshua Becker, founder of *Becoming Minimalist*

FACT: 400 percent more clothing is produced today than 20 years ago. The world now consumes 80 billion new items of clothing every year.

FACT: One trillion liters of water are used in the production of clothing ever year, making the apparel industry the second-largest consumer of the world's water supply.

FACT: The apparel industry accounts for 10 percent of the world's carbon emissions.

FACT: 85 percent of the clothes we buy end up in landfills even though the majority of it could be recycled or reused.

A Short Story on the Fashion Industry

It may come as a surprise to you, as it has to us, to learn just how much the apparel industry coupled with our clothing habits impact our environment.

Let's look at both sides of this "partnership."

The apparel industry

The end-to-end process of making the clothes and shoes we wear—from the growing and creation of fibers, through textile and product manufacturing, to the eventual shipping of product to stores—renders the apparel industry one of the most polluting in the world.

The chain of events that brings clothing to our closets does direct harm to our forests, our oceans, our soil, and our air. In addition, in many factories, unacceptably poor and often toxic working conditions negatively impact the health and well-being of the people who make our textiles, clothes, and shoes.

Here are just a few things worth understanding about this environmentally high-cost industry:

About viscose

Viscose—often called rayon—believed to be the third most commonly used textile fiber in the world, is made primarily from wood pulp, which of course comes from trees. The massive amount of viscose being created, particularly to support fast fashion, is contributing to the depletion of the world's forests.

It is estimated that approximately 30 percent of the viscose textile used in fashion is made from pulp sourced from endangered and ancient forests. In the process of making this textile, toxic chemicals are released into the air and waterways surrounding production plants.

About cotton

The production of cotton, another widely used fiber, is also problematic. Cotton not cultivated organically—which is to say the majority of the cotton produced today—requires high levels of pesticides, insecticides, and fertilizers, all of which impact soil quality and leach toxins into water. Worldwide, conventional cotton farming uses more toxic pesticides per acre than any other crop. Then there is the problem of the huge quantities of water used in the production and processing of cotton in many factories around the world.

Textile mills

Textile mills in total use some 20,000 different chemicals in their fabric manufacturing processes, many of them carcinogenic. They also generate, as waste, one-fifth of the world's industrial water pollution. Lead, mercury, and arsenic are three particularly toxic substances that are sometimes discharged by textile factories; they harm both aquatic life and the health of people whose drinking water is impacted. It doesn't help that many textile factories still use coal as fuel, producing billions of tons of soot that is released into the air, causing damaging pollution.

Clothing shipments

Finally, there is the important point noted in the chapter on Transportation, which highlights the environmental cost of all this apparel being shipped by air and sea from countries such as India, China, Bangladesh, and Vietnam.

There is the beginning of a good news story, but we need to emphasize the word *beginning*. The Global Fashion Agenda Forum, comprising many fashion manufacturers and retailers, including giants such as H&M and Adidas, recently set targets for industry collaboration on sustainability in fashion. The Apparel Impact Institute along with NRDC is working to coordinate textile mill improvement programs by identifying, funding, and scaling solutions for reducing the environmental impact of textile manufacturing.

North Americans now discard about 14 million tons of clothing and shoes every year. Yikes!!!

Fashionrevolution.org is another platform working hard to inspire major industry changes in the treatment of both workers and the environment. As is canopyplanet.org, which focuses on forest protection and in their work with the fashion industry. But there are miles to go before this industry is meaningfully transformed. And we consumers need to become a big part of the solution by virtue of the choices we make—including the things we choose not to buy.

We, the consumers

The industry is problematic—but it turns out, our own shopping habits are also a problem. **Over the last 25 years, North American purchases of clothing and shoes have more than doubled,** while our population has only grown by about 30 percent. Simply put, we just keep buying more stuff. And throwing away more stuff, more often.

We need to ask ourselves two questions:

• Why are we doing this—buying and throwing out so much?

• Where does all this discarded clothing go?

The answer to the first question: **we have been seduced.**

North Americans, like others in the developed world, have been seduced by the fashion industry and the billions of dollars being spent annually on marketing and advertising. Their objective is to convince us that we need the "newest and latest." This addiction has been supercharged by fast fashion, the newer participants in the fashion industry, who churn out new styles, very inexpensively, almost weekly. Retailers like Zara, H&M, and Uniqlo produce tens of thousands of styles a year that we consumers have come to think of as wear, wash, wear a few more times, and then toss.

The answer to the second question is disturbing. Unfortunately, most of what we throw out ends up in landfills, where it degrades and emits toxic methane and carbon gases. As noted in previous chapters, when this happens, air quality, soil, and water are all negatively impacted.

Key Takeaway:

Buy less, enjoy longer, recycle more, and push your favorite brands to adopt sustainable manufacturing processes.

Notes:

-
-
-
-
-
-
-
-
-
-
-

Reduce your clothing footprint.

Rethink our approach to the amount of new clothing we buy, and become advocates for change in the entire apparel industry.

Step 1: Build your awareness

- Go through your closet and identify everything you have purchased in the last 12 to 18 months. Ask yourself how much of what you bought you are wearing with any regularity.

- If you have kids, it's worth doing the same exercise with them.

- Spend some time on www.sustainyourstyle.org and www.fashionrevolution.org to build your understanding and learn more about the impact of fashion on our planet.

- If you want a really deep dive, check out *Fashionopolis* and *Overdressed*, two excellent books on the subject.

Step 2: Take action
Shop with intention and buy less

- Develop the habit of consciously reminding yourself of the high cost to you and the planet of "tossed fashion" before you decide on your next purchase. Can you imagine enjoying it in your wardrobe for several years? As part of this idea, take the #30WearsChallenge, which is about asking yourself if you can imagine wearing an item at least 30 times before deciding to buy it.

- Seek out clothing and shoes made with recycled or eco-friendly materials. Every day, more companies are joining the eco movement.

- Resist "of the moment" marketing trends. Shop with item longevity in mind. This is an old idea with a new twist. Think classic items that will stand the test of time.

Join the fashion reuse, recycle, donate, repurpose bandwagon

- Explore new online fashion rental services. Great ones include Haverdash, Rent the Runway, Nuuly, Gwynnie Bee, and Dresst. Even mainstream companies such as Vince and all the Urban Outfitters brands are renting clothing now. This is clearly an exciting new trend that will have many more entrants.

- Share and borrow. Shop in your friends' closets.

- Have fun at www.tulerie.com—an Airbnb for closets.

- Shop and sell clothing at secondhand, vintage, and thrift stores. Online thrift and consignment stores such as thredUP, Poshmark, and The RealReal are just a few examples of what is a great trend.

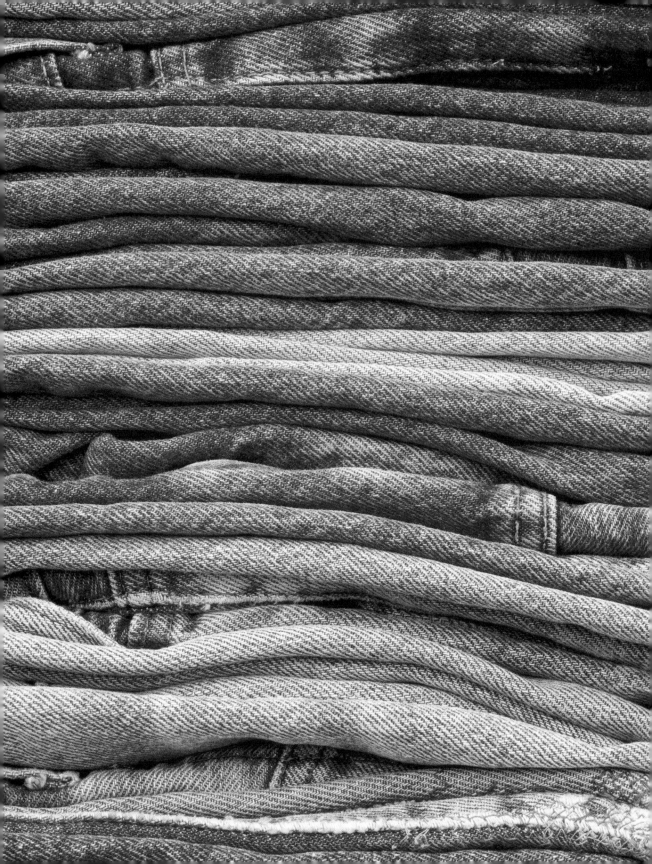

- Donate work clothes and shoes that you are no longer wearing to Dress For Success, www.dressforsuccess.org, a global nonprofit that provides professional attire for low-income women entering the workforce. While on the subject of donating, consider your local Goodwill, Salvation Army, or favorite charity after cleaning out your closet.

Clothes swapping is the new "new."

Kids love to raid their parents' closet. Do the same: have fun with friends by throwing fashion-swapping parties. Everyone invited brings clothes they aren't wearing but feel could make a great addition to someone else's wardrobe. (Include costume jewelry!)

- Recycle your old jeans. Since jeans are made from cotton, they can be recycled. The Blue Jeans Go Green program collects denim so that it can be returned to its natural fiber to be repurposed. New uses for recycled denim are now popping up, including upcycling them into housing insulation. Jeans can be dropped off or mailed to any participating retailer, including Levi's and Wrangler.

- Give clothing you can't find a home for to Terracycle, Recycle for Change, or RewearAbles, organizations whose mission is to recycle textiles and fabrics.

- Inspire tweens and teens in your neighborhood to run secondhand fashion sales. They can reach out to all their parents' friends and collect castoffs to resell for funds that can be donated to a great cause.

- Check out the Mission Statements and Guiding Principles of your favorite brands. These will tell you so much about the companies' values and their commitment to sustainability. Look for clear ambitions and specific, time-bound targets.

Become an advocate

Write the CEOs of your favorite brands and let them know that you want their full transparency on what they are doing to move toward becoming more sustainable.

Reputation is everything for fashion brands, and you can encourage a company to prioritize sustainability by reaching out on social media. Tag your favorite brands and ask them to share what they are doing to improve working conditions, waste less, and lower their carbon footprint in all aspects of their manufacturing, packaging, and distribution.

NOTE: As moving toward living sustainably is a journey for all of us, it is likely also a journey for the companies you want to influence. No organization can change instantly. Their responsibility is to be clear about what they are doing, commit to timelines, demonstrate real progress, and support, not thwart, environmental legislation.

Notes:

-
-
-
-
-
-
-
-

Our Chemical Footprint

Eventually we'll realize that if we destroy the ecosystem,
we destroy ourselves.

—Jonas Salk

You cannot talk about the environment and not talk about health.

—Catherine Flowers, Founder
Center for Rural Enterprise and Environmental Justice

FACT: More than 40,000 chemicals are used in products today, yet only a few hundred have ever been tested for safety.

FACT: Since 2009, 595 cosmetics manufacturers have reported using 88 chemicals in more than 73,000 products that have been linked to cancer, birth defects, or reproductive harm.

FACT: On average, women use 12 personal care products a day, exposing themselves to 168 chemical ingredients.

FACT: 74 million people of color in the United States live in communities affected by air pollution.

A Short Story on Chemicals

We eat them, absorb them through our skin, and breathe them in. They are in our water, our home products, our personal care and makeup, and our clothing. Synthetic chemicals are ubiquitous — they can even be found in the umbilical cords of newborns and in the bodies of polar bears in the most remote parts of the world. And without doubt they can be found in our own bodies.

It is also the case that toxic chemicals are infiltrating our soil, our air, our water systems, our marine environments, our clothing, and almost every room in our homes. We have become unwitting "partners," along with product manufacturers and industrial farmers, in creating a world with a giant chemical footprint through our purchases of products laden with harmful chemicals.

The reality is, chemicals are everywhere, and in everything. Working to understand where the risks are—and aren't—for ourselves and our planet can be a bit overwhelming. But let's give it a try.

(Friendly warning: this is a lot to absorb, so take your time. It will be worth it.)

The first important thing to understand is that the synthetic chemicals in our everyday lives come from petrochemicals.

Environmental Injustice

Chemical companies often deliberately build their factories in low-income communities, often made up of people of color. These residents aren't so much the consumers of the products being made as the victims of the pollution these factories are spewing into the air and local waterways. A few examples ...

An 85-mile corridor between Baton Rouge and New Orleans, Louisiana, home to a predominantly Black community, has come to be called Cancer Alley because the people who live near the dozens of local petrochemical plants are more than 50 times more likely than other Americans to get cancer.

There is an area in Sarnia, Canada, nicknamed Chemical Alley, which is home to many members of the Assembly of First Nations. Just 15 square miles, Chemical Alley houses factories that produce about $2.5 billion worth of petrochemicals. A UN inspector recently described Chemical Valley as "deeply disturbing with pollution levels higher than anywhere in Canada."

These are the same petrochemicals—oil and natural gas—that fuel our cars, homes, planes, and ships, and they are major contributors to climate change.

Many of the most commonly used chemicals are in fact bad for our planet and bad for our health. There is growing research that draws a direct connection between some of these chemicals and the risks of obesity, breast and prostate cancers, skin and lung irritations, thyroid problems, and ADD/ADHD.

Where are all these synthetic chemicals?

They're in and on our clothes, our home goods, and our pet products. They can be found in our food, our makeup and personal care products, our home furnishings and building products, and our gardens. It is virtually impossible to move through the day without some exposure to synthetic chemicals.

The question then becomes: Which ones should we do our best to avoid?

This is a good question, but one that is somewhat difficult to answer. More than 80,000 different chemicals are used in the products found on the market, but only a few hundred have been tested for safety. And testing is weak, at best. We will focus here on those known to be the most problematic.

Personal care and makeup products:

We all use many personal care products, including shampoo, conditioner, deodorant, tampons, soap, creams, nail polish, shaving cream, and perfume. Some of these are safe, but many include untested or harmful ingredients. Here is what is good to keep in mind. **Parabens and phthalates** pose a risk as endocrine disrupters, meaning they can interfere with the natural levels and functions of our hormone systems. They have been known to cause certain cancers, breathing problems, developmental and reproductive problems, and ADHD.

Sunscreens:

Some of our favorite sunscreen brands contain the ingredients **oxybenzone and octinoxate,** which pose a potential risk to our health and are wreaking havoc on our coral reefs. Coral reefs are essential to protect against coastline erosion, and to provide food and habitat for marine life, but coral reefs around the world are dying in front of our eyes.

Deodorants:

The deodorants we use are another everyday product we need to better understand. Many commercial deodorants contain an ingredient called **triclosan.** Triclosan is a powerful antibacterial agent that is linked to thyroid issues and has also contributed to the rise in antibiotic-resistant superbugs. In addition, triclosan cannot be filtered out during wastewater treatment, so it eventually ends up in our oceans, where it is toxic to marine life-sustaining algae.

Perfumes & Candles:

You may be surprised by the number of synthetic chemicals in the perfumes and perfumed products you use daily. Manufacturers are not required to list the ingredients that go into what they call **fragrance** as it is considered a trade secret. However, a single scent could contain anywhere from 50 to 300 synthetic chemicals. Within what is generally listed simply as "fragrance" are often many ingredients including the chemicals phthalates and parabens.

In addition, most candles are made of paraffin wax, a petroleum waste product that is chemically bleached and releases **benzene and toluene**, both known carcinogens, when burned. Best to stick with soy or beeswax candles scented with essential oils. These would have the added advantage of helping to clean the air.

For more information on which personal care, makeup, and household products contain chemicals to be avoided, consult the Haywood Healthy Home www.haywoodhealthyhome.com; the Environmental Working Group www.ewg.org; or the David Suzuki Foundation www.davidsuzuki.org.

Quick Tips for Choosing Safer

Personal Care Products

Products for Your Skin + the Sun

Avoid:

- *SPF above 50*
- *Retinyl palmitate*
- *Aerosol sprays*
- *Oxybenzone*
- *Insect repellent*

Safe to Use:

- *Hats and shade in midday sun*
- *Zinc is the best active ingredient, otherwise 3% Avobenzone*
- *SPF 30 for intense sun*
- *Broad spectrum protection*
- *Use a lot and reapply frequently*

Common Ingredients with Safety Concerns

Avoid:

- *DMDM hydantoin*
- *Diazolidinyl urea*
- *Imidazolidinyl urea*
- *Ceteareth*
- *PEG and polyethylene*

Products with "fragrance" on the label can contain hundreds of chemicals and may trigger allergic reactions.

Products for Your Kids

Diaper Cream
- *Avoid boric acid*

Baby Wipes
- *Avoid 2-bromo-2-nitropropane-1, 3-diol (bronopol)*

Toothpaste
- *Limit fluoride toothpaste for kids who might swallow it (none for kids under two)*

Avoid the Following

On Your Body
- *Triclocarban (bar soap)*
- *Triclosan (liquid soap)*

For Moisturizing
- *Retinyl palmitate or retinol in daytime skin products*

On Your Teeth
- *Triclosan in toothpaste*

On Your Lips
- *Retinyl palmitate or retinol*

On Your Nails
- *Formaldehyde or formalin in polish, hardeners, or other nail products*
- *Toluene*
- *Dibutyl phthalate (DBP)*
- *Pregnant? Skip polish*

In Your Hair
- *"Fragrance"*
- *PEG, ceteareth, and polyethylene*
- *Parabens: propyl, isopropyl, butyl, isobutyl*
- *DMDM hydantoin*

Cosmetics are poorly regulated and commonly made from untested chemicals; makers can use almost any ingredient they choose.

CHART COURTESY OF THE ENVIRONMENTAL WORKING GROUP
www.ewg.org

Chemicals and clothing

Our clothes, especially the ones that are tagged *wrinkle free*, *stain resistant*, and *water resistant*, are treated with toxic chemicals called fluorocarbons that run off into our waterways and create pollution. They are also dangerous to our health even in exquisitely tiny amounts. New clothing is sometimes finished with **formaldehyde** to prevent mildew, wrinkling, and parasites during shipping. This is particularly true if the clothing has to travel a great distance. Formaldehyde, an ever-present chemical found in a wide range of products, is a known carcinogen.

Any clothing that includes the "benefit" of being antibacterial (think workout clothing and athletic wear) may very well contain the chemical **triclosan**, which as noted above is an endocrine disrupter. NOTE: phthalates, commonly used in workout gear, have been linked to cancers and adult obesity, as well as reduced testosterone in men and women.

Another place chemicals are lurking is at your neighborhood dry cleaner's. Many use a toxic chemical solvent called **PERC** (perchloroethylene) in their cleaning process. This can stick to the dry cleaning items and end up releasing harmful gases into our cars and into our homes.

Chemicals and our food

There is a direct connection between what we eat and don't eat, our well-being, and the well-being of our environment. In particular, when it comes to our food, we need to be conscious of these three major categories of chemicals:

Pesticides used in conventional farming leave residue on the fruits and vegetables that end up on our dinner table and in our kids' lunch boxes.

Synthetic fertilizers used to boost industrial food production add excess amounts of nitrogen and phosphorus into our soil, much of which eventually runs off into our rivers and coastal waters. This runoff is directly contributing to massive marine dead zones in the Gulf of Mexico, the Great Lakes, and other important bodies of water.

Phthalates and PFAS (Per- and polyfluoroalkyl substances), as noted above, are endocrine disrupters, and can be found in plastic containers, plastic wrap, and nonstick and greaseproof food wrappers. These chemicals can and do leach into our food. Ditto BPA, which can be found in can liners and plastic water bottles and has been linked to cancer and obesity. BPA is yet another reason to ditch plastic water bottles.

Home and garden

Many home cleaning products are made with the chemicals **phosphorus, nitrogen, and ammonia,** all of which do some harm to the environment. These harsh chemicals used in our sinks and toilets, in washing machines, and in dishwashers eventually all go down the drain. Over time, residual chemicals not filtered out by the drainage systems seep into groundwater, negatively affecting wildlife, aqua life, and their supporting ecosystems.

Toxic chemicals also become part of the dust floating in and around our homes. From the flame-retardants used in sofas and many mattresses to the phthalates used in vinyl flooring and blinds and the formaldehyde in particleboard, paints, and wood flooring, products and materials in our homes are constantly shedding these chemicals as dust particles, creating potential health hazards.

Commonly used flea collars release pesticides as residues onto the fur of your pets, and these can easily rub off on anyone petting them.

Synthetic, chemical-containing fertilizers and pesticides used on lawns can be carried into our homes either by our pets or on the bottom of our shoes. These too become part of the dust we breathe.

Breathe Easy

Indoor air can be five times more polluted than outdoor air, partly because of the chemicals we unsuspectingly "invite" into our homes. The reality is that many of our household products—from carpets, to sofas, to flooring, to the very thing we sleep on—our mattresses—contain chemicals that can off-gas for years. It can sometimes be identified by "new carpet" or "new car" smell, but it can also be odorless.

Since we spend a third of our life sleeping, it makes sense to try to buy an organic mattress if possible. This has so many advantages, including eliminating the use of petroleum-based nylon, polyester, polyurethane foam, and vinyl in the creation of most mattresses and eliminating the risk to your health caused when off-gassing occurs. The good news is, there are now many companies making organic mattresses at various price points.

Finally, lawn and garden care that relies on synthetic pesticides and fertilizers can contaminate soil and kill bees, butterflies, and other critical pollinators. Don't despair— great recommendations below.

Key Takeaway:

Read labels. Encourage transparency from your favorite brands and food companies. As much as possible, opt for products—grown or created— with few or no toxic chemicals.

Notes:

-
-
-
-
-
-
-
-
-
-
-
-

A special note on PFAS —
the "forever chemicals"

One family of synthetic chemicals that is particularly troubling are the PFAS, otherwise known as "forever chemicals" because they are known to not break down in the environment. PFAS can be found in everything from non-stick pans and baking sheets to greaseproof food packaging; in takeout containers, where they can migrate to our food; in drinking water, in personal care products, stain- and water-resistant clothing, carpets, and furniture. In different ways PFAS make our lives more convenient, but this convenience comes at a price. They are indestructible.

They move around the environment easily, can enter the air we breathe, and accumulate in our bodies. They have even been found in the blood of newborns and polar bears.

Decades ago, the more common PFAS were found in products branded Teflon, Gore-Tex, and Scotchgard. Even though these particular brand name products have been phased out or reformulated, there are now thousands of chemical "cousins" in this family that are considered just as bad as their predecessors.

The more researchers and scientists learn and share about our increasingly chemical-dependent world, the more it becomes clear that we as individuals need to take back as much control as we can over what we are exposed to—for our own health, our children's, and that of the planet.

For more detailed information on toxic chemicals, consult www.nrdc.org.

Top 10 chemicals to avoid

Chemical Name	Products it's found in
Per- and polyfluoroalkyl substances (PFAS) / "Toxic Forever Chemicals"	Nonstick, waterproof, stain-resistant, greaseproof, Teflon, Gore-Tex, Scotchgard
Formaldehyde	Particleboard, paints, and wood flooring
Polybrominated Diphenyl Ethers (PBDEs) / Flame Retardants	Couch foam, mattresses, electronics, home insulation
Tetrachlorvinphos (TCVP)	Flea collars
Glyphosate, neonicotinoids (class of pesticides) / Lawn and Garden pesticides	RoundUp (glyphosate); pretreated plants (neonics)

Chemical Name	Products it's found in
Bisphenol A (BPA), Bisphenol S (BPS), Bisphenol F (BPF)	Tin can linings, soft plastics, composite dental fillings
Perchloroethylene (perc)	Dry cleaning
Phthalates	Plastics, fragrances, vinyl flooring and blinds
Triclosan	Cosmetics (often used as a preservative and so is labeled "preservative" and not "triclosan"), antimicrobial products
Benzalkonium chloride, benzethonium chloride (and many others) / "Quats"	Antibacterial hand soaps

Reduce your chemical footprint.

This shift is about becoming more aware of the chemicals we use and ingest each day and choosing products, including food products, that are better for us and for our environment.

Step 1: Build your awareness

Becoming aware of the chemical footprint all around you will inspire you to seek products that are safer for you and better for our environment.

Spend some time on www.ewg.org, www.nrdc.org, www.davidsuzuki.org, and www.safermade.net to build your knowledge about chemicals worth avoiding in everyday life.

Step 2: Take action

Become a label reader

- Read labels to better understand the chemicals you and your family are exposed to. You may need a magnifying glass, as most manufacturers don't want you looking or asking. If the writing is very small and the list is long, watch out! Rule of thumb: If you can't pronounce the chemical name, you probably don't want it in any product you buy.

- Use latest apps for scanning food ingredients or product ingredients to know what each contains.

Consider the Environmental Working Group's
list of chemicals to avoid. (www.ewg.org)

- Avoid the following when buying toilet cleaners, oven cleaners, kitchen and bathroom cleaners, or heavy-duty degreasers: hydrochloric acid, phosphoric acid, sodium or potassium hydroxide, ammonia, chlorine bleach, and ethanolamines.

- Avoid products with **quaternary ammonium** compounds, or **"quats."** These chemicals are associated with asthma and reduced fertility and birth defects in animals. Two common ones found in soaps and cleaning products are benzalkonium chloride and benzethonium chloride.

- Avoid products containing **triclosan**. Triclosan, even at low levels, has been linked to increased allergy sensitivity and disruption of thyroid function. Triclosan is an ingredient that cannot be filtered out during the wastewater treatment process. It is one of the most frequently found chemicals in water waste and is toxic to algae. Some of the most common soap brands, face washes, skin wipes, deodorants, and toothpastes use this ingredient, which is yet another reason why it is important to read labels.

Clean more cleanly

Powerful disinfectants and antimicrobial chemicals like quats are commonly found in household cleaners, despite warnings about potential serious health consequences, such as increased antibiotic resistance.

- Seek out cleaning products made with natural ingredients. There are now many cleaning brands on the market that are as effective as those containing harmful chemicals. Or try making your own cleaning products. Check online for DIY recipes for making home cleaners with everyday products you have in your kitchen, including baking soda, distilled white vinegar, lemons, and castile soap. This is often a great route to save $$.

Restock your kitchen, pantry, and bathroom

- Cook with cast iron, stainless steel, and oven-safe glass; avoid nonstick items, particularly anything with Teflon.

- Use glass in your microwave—never plastic containers, wrap, or container covers—to avoid BPA leaching into your food.

- Replace toxic cleaners with cleaners made from environmentally friendly ingredients.

- Try to eliminate as much plastic in the kitchen as possible. A good place to start: plastic food wrap, single-use plastic water bottles, plastic cups.

- Detox the products used in your shower and bathroom vanity.

- Buy clean, chemical-free shampoos, conditioners, deodorants,

Choose Organic Tampons

Organic tampons are made free of dyes, rayon, chlorine, and artificial fragrance and often come without the plastic applicator. The average woman will use as many as 16,000 tampons in her life, so avoiding the chemicals and choosing applicator-free really does make a difference.

and makeup. Look for products that don't contain parabens, phthalates, or sodium lauryl sulfate.

• Try to avoid personal care products with BHA (beta hydroxyl acid) and BHT (butylated hydroxytoluene), formaldehyde-releasing preservatives, parabens, parfum (aka fragrance), triclosan, PEG (polyethylene glycol) compounds, petrolatum, siloxanes, and sodium laureth sulfate.

• Purchase makeup that is free of synthetic fragrances, is mineral-based, or is made from natural oils. Buying organic products will greatly reduce your exposure to chemical toxins and be better for our ecosystems.

• A special note on lipstick: Women typically apply lipstick many times a day. If you unconsciously lick your lips or drink and eat food while wearing lipstick, it will end up in your stomach. Some of the potentially dangerous petroleum-based chemicals found in your favorite brands could include: aluminum, cadmium, chromium, lead, and manganese.

Detox your closet

- Avoid buying clothing that is marked *drip dry, easy care, stain resistant, water resistant, or sweat reducing,* as these contain harmful chemicals.

- Avoid dry cleaners that use the toxic chemical PERC (perchloroethylene) in the cleaning process. If you are using a standard dry cleaner, do not allow them to put plastic bags over the clothing as this holds in the chemicals used in the cleaning process and they will off-gas in your car and at home.

Go for chemical-free gardening

Opt for organic pesticides and insecticides for your lawn or garden, as the synthetic chemicals in commercial pesticides and insecticides do get absorbed into the soil, groundwater, and any food you are growing. In addition, water absorbed into the ground often becomes runoff and ends up in places where it can harm fish and animals. It can even come out of our kitchen taps after it has contaminated the rivers, lakes, and streams that are the source of our drinking water. NOTE: The chemicals in these products can get trekked into your house from your shoes when you come inside. They can even waft in through open windows.

- Cross Roundup and other weed killers off your shopping list! Among other harmful impacts, weed killers are toxic to the milkweed plant on which monarch butterflies lay their eggs. These herbicides are devastating populations of butterflies, bees, and other pollinator species.

- When buying plants, make sure they have not been pretreated with pesticides.

- Opt for organic pesticides and insecticides. (LD: Worth knowing is that some pests, such as snails and slugs, can be controlled by simply handpicking them, and dropping them into soapy water. Early morning is best for this activity.)

- Encourage your elected officials to pass city and town ordinances to reduce pesticide and herbicide spraying on public lawns, gardens, and parks.

- Consider letting your lawn grow a bit longer, leaving blooming clover for the bees to enjoy.

- Plant marigolds. They are charming, easily affordable, and do double duty as a natural bug repellent.

Keep your pet safe

- Explore nonchemical pet products. There are many pet products on the market that offer an alternative to the chemical-based flea and tick control collars regularly used.

- Use a chemical-free soap to wash your pet.

A Note on Greenwashing

This is a term used to describe the actions of a company that, in an attempt to win over the customer, makes a product or service sound more environmentally friendly than it actually is. This is accomplished in a number of ways, including visuals on the label—think a green pasture and a child chasing a butterfly—or the use of words on packaging that are fuzzy and don't really mean anything, such as natural, clean, eco, *or* free of harmful ingredients *(while the product still includes ingredients that are not environmentally sound). Ironically, the more customers demand environmentally friendly products, the more widespread greenwashing has become. Buyer beware. Best to look for products clearly labeled organic. This is an actual, government-approved certification with clear requirements.*

- Wash your pet's bedding regularly in hot, soapy water.

- Vacuum and wipe down pet-frequented surfaces, including any furniture they regularly cuddle on or under.

- Consider putting beneficial nematodes—worms that eat flea larvae—in the soil where your pet is likely to frolic. Find them in garden supply stores or online.

Be a careful car owner

- Practice good car maintenance to reduce the risk of leaking oil, coolant, antifreeze, and other liquids containing nasty chemicals. These often end up being carried by rainwater or hose water down driveways or through parking lots and into groundwater.

- If possible, choose a car wash over hosing down when you wash your car. Car wash companies are required to drain their wastewater into sewer systems, where the water is treated for all the bad stuff before being discharged. Car washes are also more efficient in terms of water usage than hand washing your car at home.

Build or renovate safely

If you are building or renovating, keep in mind that many building products and many home design products are made with toxic chemicals.

- Consult www.homefree.healthybuilding.net for guidance on products that are best to avoid or those that are free of toxic chemicals, including paints, flooring, drywall, cabinetry, and countertops.

- Look for products approved by reliable certifiers, including International Living Future Institute, Cradle to Cradle Products, Innovation Institute, Green Seal, and BlueGreen Alliance.

- Buy from companies and manufacturers that take part in the Health Product Declaration Collaborative. They disclose everything—including potential chemicals of concern—that goes into what they make and sell.

Become an advocate

We should not have to scour labels with a magnifying glass and the latest label app to be sure the products we are buying are fully safe for ourselves and the planet.

- Call on your local, state, provincial, and federal governments to demand label transparency and that toxic chemicals be banned.

- Petition your favorite retailers to stop selling products that pose serious health and environmental risks, including furniture or clothing treated with flame-retardant chemicals or garden products that include glyphosate.

- Follow and support efforts by NRDC and davidsuzuki.org to ban "bee-killing neonics," a class of chemical pesticide widely used in the US and Canada, and described by the National Center for Scientific Research in France as 5,000 to 10,000 times more toxic than DDT. Study after study connects neonicotinoid pesticides to the collapse of our bee populations, on which we as humans have relied for some 9,000 years. Neonics are also harming birds, butterflies, aquatic ecosystems, and humans. **Neonics are considered an environmental "triple threat" because they are toxic, highly mobile, and long-lasting.** They can be found in our water, our soil, and our food. Shockingly, neonic residue is in 86 percent of honey in North America, and can also be found in conventionally grown apples, cherries, strawberries, and baby food! The residue is actually *inside* the fruit and veggies, and therefore cannot be washed off. Wow!

Talk about Ahead of the Curve

Dr. Bronner's, the American producer of organic soaps and personal care products, has been espousing green values since 1858, when this family-owned soap business first began. "Treat the Earth like Home" is their motto, and this company has been walking this talk for over 150 years.

Dr. Bronner products, including their signature castile soap made from vegetable oil, are effective for a wide variety of uses. The soap is so versatile it can be used from your shower to your kitchen floor and so much in between. The company is also committed to renewable power, postconsumer recycled packaging, and sourcing from organic farms.

*Pictured here —3 from the left — John Adams, Founder of NRDC;
and one from the right — Laurie David, 2019*

A Word on Being an Advocate

Not everything that is faced can be changed, but nothing can be changed until it's faced.

—James Baldwin

This may well be one of the most important pages in this book. You have power! And working on behalf of the environment and fighting for environmental justice is a great way to use it. There is no shortage of environmental causes that need your help, from addressing contaminated drinking water to fighting illegal waste dumping, to highlighting the unequal environmental price being paid by BIPOC communities, to national and international efforts on climate. Pick your issue and join the fight.

Use Your Social Media Platforms

Every single CEO today, and every single individual running for office, is keenly aware of what we as consumers and voters are saying about them on their social media platforms. They are plugged in, and they know when a post or video we create gains attention and goes viral. And that awareness can motivate positive change.

So, speak up! Write, post, share, tag, inspire your friends and colleagues, and amplify the voices of others. Make phone calls, join campaigns. March. Be a squeaky wheel. Spread the word. Get involved. If you don't, other self-interested voices, denying our environmental crises, will fill the void.

When you read an article about an injustice, share it. Educate your friends. When you receive a product wrapped in too much disposable plastic and paper, when you discover your favorite brand contains a toxic chemical, when you check a label and find it impossible to decipher, when you visit a corporate website only to discover there is no meaningfully articulated environmental strategy, tweet about it, and post images on your own social platforms and the company's social platforms. While you are at it—consider shining a spotlight on those companies taking real initiative and leading the pack on environmental action.

Write letters directly to CEOs. In today's environment, every good CEO will want to know what their customers are saying, and they are competitive with each other. A letter can have huge impact, particularly if you also copy your elected officials. Let corporate leaders know that you will continue to support them only if they take real action to become environmentally conscious. Let them know what you want them to change and that you are sharing your views with everyone in your network.

Know, too, that corporations are filled with employees who also care about the environment. When you speak up on social platforms or in writing, you help to augment their voices.

The same is true for your elected officials or those hoping to get elected for the first time. Use the power of your voice on social platforms and in letters; and bring your entire network of friends and colleagues to the cause. Make the environment a key voting issue. In the United States, consult the League of Conservation Voters www.lcv.org, in Canada, the Climate Action Network climateactionnetwork.ca, to see the environmental voting record of anyone you are considering voting for.

It is worth noting that for over 25 years, the League of Conservation Voters has released an extensively researched report highlighting candidates, regardless of party affiliation, who directly support the environment or who consistently side against the environment.

Join an Environmental Group

Another high-impact way to use your influence is by joining a local or national environmental group. The best of these groups—and there are many—are using some combination of science, specific expertise, and the law to lobby for legislation to advance our efforts to protect both our environment and our health. When you join one of these groups, you help to amplify their efforts and support the advancement of their work. In exchange, they will keep you well-informed on the issues you care about and help you to channel your energy in directions that will have real impact.

See the Appendix for a list of some of the environmental groups you might want to consider.

Adopt a Community Issue

If there is an environmental issue being addressed in your community—get involved. Alternatively, consider other communities that could use your help. Often it is the communities with the fewest resources and the least influence who are most taken advantage of by polluting industries.

For example, the chemical and energy industries disproportionately locate in BIPOC and low-income communities. It is therefore so valuable to connect with and support the leaders in these communities who are, against the odds, fighting the fight. Whether it's stopping a pipeline on Native land or helping a community demand access to clean drinking water, your involvement can make a big difference.

One way to get involved with communities facing industrial pollution, water contamination, and crumbling infrastructure is to support the Environmental Justice Health Alliance (ej4all.org). EJHA works directly with local affiliates to address the outsized pollution burdens faced by low-income communities disproportionately made up of BIPOC.

Be a Role Model

As you learn more and become more committed to protecting the environment, it changes who you are and what you will accept. As you act and share what you know, you inspire others to do the same. You become a role model. There is actually a psychological term to describe this phenomenon: *behavioral contagion.* Sometimes also called *social contagion*, it is a type of social influence. It refers to the tendency for a person to copy the behavior of others whom they have been exposed to and admire.

"I hope people will think about the consequences of the small choices they make each day. What do you buy? Where was it made? Did it harm the environment? If everybody makes ethical choices, we start moving toward a better world."

—Jane Goodall

Our Paper Footprint

I took a walk in the woods and came out taller than the trees.

—Henry David Thoreau

FACT: 15 billion trees are cut down each year; only 4 billion are planted.

FACT: Paper accounts for 25 percent of landfill waste and 33 percent of municipal waste. (theworldcounts.com)

FACT: The average person in North America uses, in one form or another, 474 pounds of paper every year.

FACT: 16 billion paper cups—made from 6.5 million trees—are used for coffee every year.

The Short Story on Paper

We rarely, if ever, think about climate change and other environmental damage when we are filling our shopping carts with paper towels, facial tissues, or toilet paper; and likely even less when we are picking up our morning cup of coffee or using paper cups, paper shopping bags, or all that holiday wrapping paper. Ditto when standing at the photocopier. Paper is just a ubiquitous item in our lives and one we generally think of as having little or no value and totally disposable.

The reality is that paper has many impacts on our planet. Every step of the process, from logging to pulping to manufacturing to eventual trashing, puts some level of stress on the climate, on our communities, and on our ecosystems.

Logging

Let's start with where paper comes from—our forests.
The health and future of forests is inextricably tied to our own health and future. Forests, from the lush tropical rain forests of South America and Borneo to the majestic boreal forest that crowns the Earth's northern hemisphere, are home to species found nowhere else on Earth as well as to Indigenous peoples who have both stewarded and relied on these forests for millennia. Forests are also critical allies in the fight against climate change, as they absorb planet-warming carbon dioxide from the air.

As the world's demand for paper has grown, so too has industrial logging of our forests. Often, this logging involves clear-cutting centuries-old forests that will take many human lifetimes to return—if they ever do. *Three billion* trees are logged for packaging alone every year, and some of them come from ancient and endangered forests. Think cardboard boxes, shoe boxes, boxes for beauty products, and so much more.

Toilet paper may represent one of the most egregious and wasteful causes of forest loss. The largest US toilet paper brands drive a dangerous tree-to-toilet "pipeline" that is contributing to an unsustainable loss of trees, including the boreal forest in Canada. This is one of the few remaining and largest intact wildernesses in the world and one of the world's most precious resources for mitigating climate change. The Canadian boreal forest is home to boreal caribou and billions of migratory birds seen in backyards across North America each spring and fall. It is a treasure!

Fortunately, there are alternatives to sending old-growth forests to a short-lived fate in a bathroom or as a cup for coffee. Instead of using virgin forest fiber, which is made directly from trees, companies could use alternative fibers. These alternative materials have a fraction of the environmental impact. For example, toilet paper made from recycled content has one-third the carbon footprint of toilet paper made from virgin forest fiber.

Paper Production

Losing the trees is just one part of the problem. The trees taken from the forest are turned into pulp, and that pulp is turned into paper in a process that itself has severe environmental impacts. The paper-making process discharges greenhouse gases into the air and creates toxic wastewater runoff. Of particular concern are chlorine-based bleaches used to make paper whiter. While there are now some restrictions on the kinds of bleach that paper companies can use, even the new bleaches release toxins into the air and water, which can contaminate our drinking water and the fish we eat.

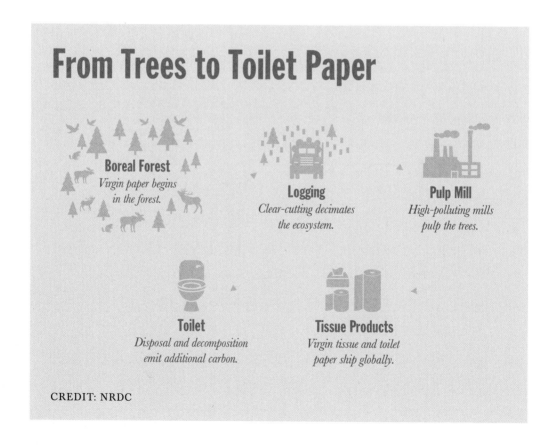

From Trees to Toilet Paper

Boreal Forest
Virgin paper begins in the forest.

Logging
Clear-cutting decimates the ecosystem.

Pulp Mill
High-polluting mills pulp the trees.

Toilet
Disposal and decomposition emit additional carbon.

Tissue Products
Virgin tissue and toilet paper ship globally.

CREDIT: NRDC

On paper waste

Paper accounts for up to 25 percent of total waste in the United States and close to one-third of all waste in Canada. Of all the paper that is discarded, approximately 60 percent is recycled, which is essentially the beginning of a good news story. The problem is that the remainder, which is not recycled, is still a lot of paper. Some of the paper that is more challenging to recycle includes paper that is wax coated or has absorbed food waste—for example, coated juice and cereal boxes, coated paper cups, milk cartons, ice-cream cartons, soiled pizza boxes, magazines laminated with plastic. Even store receipts that have a plastic coating.

This unrecyclable paper ends up in landfills, and that is where the big problem occurs. Landfills are the third-largest source of human-generated methane emissions in the US, and decomposing paper is one of the most significant sources of landfill methane.

NOTE: Not all recycled paper is of equal value in terms of environmental advantage. Postconsumer recycled paper, which uses fiber made from paper that was used, recycled, and then turned into something else, is the most sustainable kind of recycled material. Pre-consumer recycled paper, which is made from manufacturing scraps but hasn't ever actually been used by consumers, is better than virgin forest wood fiber but doesn't have the same benefits as postconsumer recycled material. It's a subtle but important difference! Generally, a product made with recycled paper is marked as such.

Certification systems like the Forest Stewardship Council (FSC) and the Sustainable Forestry Initiative (SFI) confirm with a product stamp which paper products come from responsibly managed forests.

Paper products made from postconsumer recycled material help to divert paper from landfills and reduce harmful emissions. If companies that are currently making paper products and using virgin pulp were instead to invest in increasing the capacity and quality of their recycling infrastructure, we would be able to turn even more waste paper into new products.

Key Takeaway:

Retrain your brain. Connect paper with trees. Less paper, less virgin paper, and more postconsumer recycled paper = less destruction of our forests, our air, and our water.

Dear Mr./Ms. President

Walking down Costco's tissue aisle gives you a small glimpse into what is happening with toilet tissue. Charmin, Bounty, and Costco's own Kirkland toilet paper are all made with 100 percent virgin forest fiber, sourced in part from the climate-critical Canadian boreal forest. The boreal is the most carbon-dense forest in the world, and in Canada it is being clear-cut at a rate of one million acres a year to make lumber, paper, and—perhaps most egregiously—throwaway tissue products.

Further research will show this is true for almost all companies selling toilet tissue. Look no further than Walmart, Target, or your favorite chain grocery store.

Throwaway tissue products don't have to destroy forests. In fact, NRDC and Stand.earth's 2019 scorecard "The Issue with Tissue" listed many tissue products available today that are made from much climate-friendlier substances, such as recycled content. According to the Environmental Paper Network's Paper Calculator 4.0, tissue products made from 100 percent recycled content have one-third the carbon footprint of those made from 100 percent virgin forest fiber.

Write the CEO of your favorite retailer and let her/ him/them know that you will not support a retailer who continues to sell toilet tissue made from wood taken from ancient, irreplaceable forests.

www.environmentalpaper.org

Rethink your paper habit.

This shift is about lessening our paper usage, particularly any paper made with virgin wood; using postconsumer recycled paper products as much as possible; and using a recycle bin for all reusable paper waste.

Step 1: Build your awareness

As you did with plastic, start your mind-shift by taking stock of all the paper you use or toss during any given day. Think about the kitchen, the bedroom, the bathroom. Then think about the paper waste you experience at your work environment, after shopping trips, and after stops at your favorite coffee shop and lunch spot.

Check out us.fsc.org or www.canopyplanet.org to learn more about the relationship between our paper usage and our planet.

Pizza Pizza

The popularity of pizza has exploded in the last several decades. All that pizza comes in cardboard boxes. Unfortunately, once these boxes absorb cheese and grease, they can no longer be recycled.

The good news is that World Centric, a company that produces compostable products from plant-based materials, has developed a plant-based pizza box that is fully compostable. We need to pressure our favorite pizza joints to switch to these environmentally friendlier boxes.

Step 2: Take action

- Consider NRDC's Toilet Paper Sustainability Scorecard when you buy toilet tissue. This scorecard looks at factors including the product's percentage of postconsumer recycled content, whether the bleach used in manufacturing is toxic, and if the tissue is made from virgin forest fiber. Notice that the largest brands, for example Procter & Gamble's Charmin, received an F grade because, sadly, they are made entirely from virgin forest fiber.

Toilet Paper Sustainability Scorecard

A	B	D	F
GREEN FOREST	Marcal 1000	365 Sustainably Soft	Charmin Ultra Soft
365 Bath Tissue	Marcal small steps	Cottonelle ULTRA ComfortCare	KIRKLAND Signature
NATURAL VALUE Earth First		Scott 1000	Angel Soft
seventh GENERATION		Scott ComfortPlus	QUILTED NORTHERN
TRADER JOE'S Bath Tissue		TRADER JOE'S Super Soft Bath Tissue	up&up soft & strong
cascades Fluff ENVIRO			

CREDIT: NRDC

Look for ways to reduce your use of paper

• Use a reusable mug rather than daily disposable paper coffee cups.

• Replace paper towels with a basket or container of small cloth towels that you keep beside any sink or where your paper towels would normally be. (HMR: I was definitely a paper towel addict until I was inspired by an image I saw of towels in a basket in what looked to be a busy kitchen. Since the day I implemented this new habit at home, I have never looked back. I don't miss the paper at all—I wash the towels in cold water—and feel great about it all.)

• Replace parchment paper used in baking with silicone baking mats.

• Consider e-vites rather than physical cards for invitations.

• Save old T-shirts for wiping down windows and cleaning the car.

• Use re-giftable wraps, leftover fabric, old scarves, or the pages of a magazine instead of new gift wrap.

• Fall in love with cloth napkins. It's worth noting that cloth napkins end up being far less expensive than the constant replacement of paper ones. And the bonus is that they look great on your table. If possible, try to find organic cotton or linen, or natural fibers like bamboo. (NOTE: It is so not necessary to iron cloth napkins. Even with a few wrinkles, they will look charming on the table.)

• When eliminating paper isn't possible or desirable, look for postconsumer recycled material or sustainable alternative fibers, such as wheat straw or sustainable bamboo. Today paper is even being made with recycled cotton.

Be paper smart at the office (home or work)

- Use postconsumer recycled paper in your printer and print double-sided when possible.

- While we're on the topic of printing: consider recycling your toner cartridges by dropping them off at a local supply store. If you can, inspire the same action at your office.

Green your coffee habit

- If you are going to a coffee shop, bring a reusable mug. Like water bottles, there are many great designs on the market. Paper coffee cups are often harder to recycle because of their plastic coating and residual liquid. Just be careful to pick a mug or container meant for hot liquid.

- Replace your paper coffee filters with a washable, reusable one.

- Reconsider the coffee pod. These pods are proving difficult to recycle and are piling up in landfills at alarming rates.

- As an aside: Look for the fair trade label on your coffee bag. This confirms that the company's farmers are using environmentally sound practices. It also means the company pays them a fair price and provides fair working conditions.

Delist yourself from mailings and catalogs

Take a good look at what you get in your mailbox. Unsubscribe from anything you regularly get sent but don't use or read, including catalogs and information circulars. You can often do this online or with a simple phone call. Our experience suggests this is a very satisfying activity.

Become an advocate

Write to express your dissatisfaction with companies that continue to use virgin paper for their products. Any paper product not clearly marked as made with postconsumer or recycled material is by definition made with virgin paper. When CEOs start hearing that their customers are unhappy, they act. Post your letter on social media. (See draft letter in the Appendix.)

- Let the publishers of your favorite magazines and newspapers know that you would appreciate their using ethically sourced paper. Newspapers and magazines add up to a lot of daily trash—not just what we buy but also because of unsold copies or what are called "overruns." All unsold copies of magazines at the grocery store, drugstore, or bookshop end up being shredded, amounting to tons and tons of trash.

- Demand that Procter & Gamble stop felling trees from Canadian boreal forests to make toilet paper.

- Encourage the stores you frequent to provide digital rather than paper receipts. As an aside, 90 percent of paper receipts are printed on a paper coated with the chemical BPA, which is considered toxic and an endocrine disrupter. (You can read more on this in the chapter on chemicals.)

- Vote with your dollars. When possible, spend your money with businesses that prioritize and practice corporate environmental responsibility. Corporate websites are a great place to learn about an organization's values and commitment to the environment.

- Demand that your retailer of choice replace Charmin, Bounty, and its own Kirkland toilet paper with toilet tissue made from sustainable papers.

- Express your concern with, and pull back your dollars from, companies that use virgin paper to make products or packaging.

- Ask your local pizza joint to consider switching to a fully compostable pizza box.

- Support reforesting projects and initiatives.

- Subscribe to Canopy's newsletter (canopyplanet.org), which will keep you informed on campaigns to protect forests and provide resources for supporting eco-friendly paper brands and packaging.

- Use your voice. Even protected areas need protecting. In the last few years, we've seen the United States government mount a concerted attack on conservation efforts and protected lands. This can happen in any country if there are not vigilant and determined efforts to save our "special places."

- Add your support to the Pack4Good Campaign (canopyplanet.org), which has the goal of making all packaging free of ancient and endangered trees by 2022.

- Support tree planting programs. 1t.org is a global initiative committed to reforestation by planting 1 trillion trees worldwide, launched by the United Nations environment program. It has gleaned support from a wide range of climate activists including tech entrepreneur Marc Benioff and leading conservationist Jane Goodall.

Notes:

-
-
-
-

Our Water Footprint

Water is the driving force of all nature.

—Leonardo da Vinci

FACT: The World Health Organization estimates that by 2025 half of the world's population will be living in water-stressed areas.

FACT: Global water demand has increased by over 600 percent in the last 100 years.

FACT: The average person in the United States and Canada uses close to 90 gallons of water a day.

FACT: Household leaks in the United States account for nearly a TRILLION gallons of wasted water every year.

A Short Story on Water

Water is essential to life—human life, plant life, animal life. Most of us living in the Western world think of water as endlessly available and essentially free. Think again.

The truth is that clean, abundant, and precious water is one of our most threatened natural resources.

Although water covers 70 percent of the planet, less than 1 percent of it is available to support our homes, farm fields, forests, and businesses. This means it is essential for us to understand and address the five key factors putting unsustainable stress on our water supply systems. These factors are: climate change, an increasing demand for water, our increasing affection for meat, water waste, and water pollution.

A few words on each of these ...

Climate change

It is definitely getting hotter. Meteorologists say 2020 is the hottest year on record, on the heels of five of the hottest years ever recorded. Global warming is causing unexpected, escalating changes in our climate systems, resulting, among other things, in more frequent and longer periods of drought, extreme heat waves, fires, and intense flooding. The hotter the planet the more we have heat-driven evaporation just when we need more water for agriculture, for our forests, for people, and for animals.

While we are on the subject of global warming—a related and important additional factor is that rising temperatures are creating increased humidity as hotter air holds more moisture. This too is dangerous to people, agriculture, and our environmental systems.

Increasing demand for water

Two factors are driving increased demand for water around the world. The first is population growth. The world's population is predicted to grow from 7 billion today to 10 billion by 2050, and this following the population explosion of the 20th century, when the population grew from 1.6 billion to 6 billion. Put simply, within a 150-year period, we have increased by 8.4 billion the number of people requiring a constant supply of fresh, clean water. The fact that they require it doesn't of course mean that everyone is getting it. 785 million people worldwide lack access to safe water today. 2 billion people lack access to proper sanitation.

So ... finite water, way more people, more pollution.

Our love affair with meat

Over the past 50 years, meat production has more than quadrupled. The world now produces more than 320 million tons of meat every year to meet demand. Livestock have a large environmental impact—not least because they are huge consumers of water. To produce one pound of beef requires 1,799 gallons of water.

Water leaks

A staggering amount of water is lost each day in cities from water leaks—the average household leaks nearly 10,000 gallons of water every year. Think dripping taps, hoses, water that is left running, etc. (Just think of the money we are literally pouring down the drain!) Water leaks from both commercial and residential sources are wasting this precious resource.

Water pollution

As demand for food, energy, and manufactured products grows, we have more agricultural and industrial chemicals seeping into and tainting our water supply. Decaying infrastructure in our cities, which includes things like lead pipes, can also make our water dangerous to drink. Add to this the disturbing fact that

80 percent of the world's wastewater is dumped, largely untreated, back into our rivers, our streams, our oceans, our earth.

Many of the goods we buy every day—and especially much of our clothing, including "fast fashion"—are manufactured using processes that dump toxic dyes and chemicals into water systems.

Key Takeaway:

Water is a precious resource. We should be doing everything possible to respect, treasure, and protect it.

Use water carefully.

This shift is about becoming more aware of how much water we use and waste on a daily basis, both directly and indirectly; and about taking actions that make us more respectful stewards of this invaluable resource.

Step 1: Build your awareness

- For one week, be conscious of how much water you use and when you use it over the course of each day. Include your family members in this activity and share notes at the end of the week. Identify where and how water usage could be cut back. Remember to consider such things as watering your lawn, washing your car, the number of times you run your washing machine and dishwasher, time in the shower, taps left running, etc.

- Once you have taken actions, including some of those identified below, read your water bills carefully to assess how your usage and costs change as you change your habits.

H_2O

Aging lead pipe infrastructures in communities, schools, and homes are responsible for lead leaching into our drinking water. Lead in water is particularly harmful to babies and young children because no level of lead ingestion is acceptable. It can also be a health hazard for adults and lead to increased blood pressure, incidence of hypertension, and decreased kidney function. Things worth considering:

- *If possible get your water tested for lead levels.*
- *If your water is at risk, consider installing a water filter.*
- *Do not drink warm or hot water from the tap as this increases the potential for lead to leach.*
- *Keep a filtered water pitcher in your fridge for regular drinking water.*
- *Use filtered water for baby formula.*

Step 2: Take action

Be shower smart

- Be conscientious about the amount of time you spend in the shower.

- Consider upgrading your showerhead to one that conserves water. A 20-minute shower with an older, high-flow showerhead could use as much as 100 gallons of water. But a 10-minute shower with an energy-saving WaterSense showerhead consumes no more than 20 gallons.

- Want to really go for it? Set a timer to get into the 7-minute shower groove.

Turn the tap off while you brush your teeth or shave

- It's hard to believe, but you can save a lot of water if you turn the tap off while you are brushing your teeth or shaving. Imagine the impact if everyone took the time to do this!

Water your lawn less often and more efficiently

- Watering in the early morning or late evening will reap benefits in how much water actually soaks into the ground versus evaporates into the air. Midday, when the sun is at its hottest, is the least efficient time to water your lawn.

- No matter where you live, consider replacing part or all of your lawn with less thirsty, native plantings. This adds to biodiversity and cuts down on the need for so much watering.

- Add an automatic shutoff nozzle to the end of your hose. You will save five gallons of water per minute as you go to and from the tap controlling the flow. A nozzle is especially helpful when washing your car.

- Sweep instead of hosing down walkways and driveways. This not only saves water but can reduce the amount of polluted runoff making its way into local waterways.

Be a smart dish and clothes washer

- If you have a dishwasher, run it only when it is full. By the way, although it may sound counterintuitive, dishwashers are more efficient than hand washing.

Levi's Leads

It turns out the process for making your jeans uses an enormous amount of water, from growing the cotton through to the manufacturing and "finishing" process. Finishing is what gives them that soft feeling of comfort we all love. But this last process, which creates the "broken-in" style, comes at a huge environmental cost.

Levi's took a hard look at this and did something about it. They put their minds to redesigning how they finish their jeans and came up with a powerful new approach. Instead of washing denim with water and fabric softener to create that worn-in feel, they tumble jeans with bottle caps and golf balls, lowering by 96 percent the amount of water used during this final stage.

To date, Levi's has saved more than 3 billion liters of water thanks to their innovations, and today more than 67 percent of all their products are made with this Water<Less process. BTW: Levi's recommends washing jeans only after 10 wearings!

- When hand washing dishes or pots, turn the water off while you scrub.

- Wait until you have a full load of laundry before using the washing machine, and consider setting the temperature to warm rather than hot. This cleans just as well and uses half the energy. Cold is even better!

- Look for EnergyStar or WaterSense labels when buying new appliances and fixtures. Worth knowing: Front-loading clothes washers use one-third of the water and energy of the old top-loading machines. Some utilities provide rebates and other incentives for upgrading to high-efficiency appliances. Check it out with your energy provider.

- Wash your denim jeans less. Levi's recommends washing jeans after 10 wearings!

- Hang up and reuse damp towels if they are still clean.

Fix leaky faucets and toilets

- It is amazing how much water is wasted when household faucets drip, drip, drip. A leak that produces one drop of water a second wastes more than 3,000 gallons a year. That's the equivalent of 180 showers!

- As many as one in five toilets may have a leak. Consider dye testing. Place a few drops of food coloring in your toilet tank, then come back 15 minutes later. Color in the toilet bowl is a telltale sign you have a leak.

- If you own a house, consider installing rain barrels at the foot of your home's downspouts—collect the rainwater and use it to water your trees, pots, or garden. You will be saving money and watering your garden with fresh rainwater—how great is that?!

Eat more plant-based meals

- Save water by making a few of your meals fully vegetarian. As noted above, it takes 1,799 gallons of water to produce a single pound of beef, 519 gallons for a pound of chicken, but only 39 gallons to produce the same amount of veggie. Lentils, chickpeas (think hummus), edamame, and green peas are fantastic protein sources for those concerned about getting enough protein.

- Having a party? Consider serving a vegetarian feast. (See our list of exceptional vegetarian cookbooks in the Appendix.)

Scoop the poop

- Picking up pet waste keeps bacteria-laden poop from running into storm drains and water supplies.

Become an advocate

- Call or write your elected officials and demand that they: (i) enforce and strengthen water quality safeguards; (ii) hold industries accountable for pollution; and (iii) invest in replacing aging lead pipe infrastructure in your community.

- Support the **Environmental Health Justice Alliance** to help economically disadvantaged communities dealing with contaminated drinking water. This is a national group working to protect some of America's most hard-hit communities from industrial pollution, water contamination, and infrastructure neglect. BIPOC are disproportionately the people living in these communities. Sign up for their campaign emails, follow them on social media, amplify their message, make a donation. ej4all.org

Notes:

-
-
-

Our Transportation Footprint

The eyes of all future generations are upon you.

—Greta Thunberg

FACT: One gas-powered car emits, on average, five tons of carbon dioxide per year. That's equivalent to burning 5,500 pounds of coal.

FACT: A container ship can out-pollute 50 million cars.

FACT: Almost 30 percent of all greenhouse gases are created by transportation.

FACT: Traffic areas around schools—where vehicles are often left idling—show significantly higher pollution inside school buildings.

A Short Story on Fossil Fuel-Based Transportation

Transportation is a major contributor to carbon emissions, and reducing them is essential to tackling our climate crisis. Cars, trucks, planes, and ships, all of which run on fossil fuels, now produce more planet-warming pollution than power plants.

Governments can help by developing smarter and cleaner public transit infrastructure (i.e., trains and buses that quickly and conveniently connect people with their destinations, enhanced walking and bike paths) and by incentivizing the adoption of electric vehicles; but individuals also have an important role to play in reducing transportation-based carbon emissions. Let's break this down.

Cars and trucks

The story on cars and trucks is simple. Cars and trucks account for nearly one-fifth of US greenhouse gas emissions. Tailpipe pollution is also among the top causes of smog, which, when breathed in, can cause immediate or long-term respiratory problems even when inhaled at very low levels. People in communities of color are, once again, disproportionately exposed to higher levels of this air pollution based on where they live and work.

The sooner we transition to clean-fuel cars and trucks, the better for our planet and all its people. The good news is that the cost of electric cars is coming down at an exponential rate and all major car companies have made big commitments to supporting this transition.

Notwithstanding the ambition of going electric, even the most aggressive projections suggest it will likely be close to 2050 before we fully say goodbye to the combustion engine. Interestingly, during the coronavirus pandemic, many people realized how life could be improved if we reduced our dependence on cars altogether. Cities have had to quickly increase walking and biking space—and people have responded very positively.

It was inspiring, in the midst of the loss and grief wrought by the pandemic, to see the skies clearing, hear the songbirds, see fishes and dolphins swimming in rivers and estuaries they had abandoned. So, imagine replacing parking lots, bumper-to-bumper traffic, and exposure to climate- and people-harming air pollution with more pocket parks, green spaces, bike lanes, farmers' markets, and pedestrian paths.

Air travel

For people who fly for business and pleasure, air travel is a big part of their carbon footprint. Our collective flying time has grown so much that just prior to COVID-19, greenhouse gas emissions from air travel had reached a level that surprised even the airline industry. The answer to this, in addition to aviation industry advances in lowering fossil fuel consumption and dependency, rests with being judicious in our air travel decisions.

One bright light emerging from the COVID-19 pandemic is how much we have learned about our ability to communicate digitally—particularly for business. While face-to-face meetings will still be important, the hope is that all of us will be more intentional about when it makes sense to fly and when a digital connection is just as effective. Even a 25 percent reduction in business travel will have a significant impact.

On ships

Ships are another major contributor to our increasing carbon emissions. Over 90 percent of world trade is carried across the world's oceans by some 90,000 marine vehicles burning the dirtiest fuel on the market. At present, carbon dioxide emissions from oceangoing vessels are completely unregulated.

World trade has increased dramatically over the last 15 years, with much of what is consumed in North America coming from distant locations including China, India, Japan, Bangladesh, Vietnam, and Korea.

Ships also create environmental stress when they are in dock. Many industrial marine ports operate next door to low-income residential neighborhoods, schools, and playgrounds. The residents of these communities face extraordinarily high health risks from the air pollution. Often these are communities of color, a fact that yet again raises environmental justice concerns.

Marine ports have been expanding to accommodate the growing traffic spurred by our increasing demand for goods, particularly fast fashion. Activities in and around ports are releasing so much pollution they can out-pollute larger sources of harmful emissions such as power plants and refineries. Not only do the ships themselves pollute while in port, so do the many diesel trucks coming back and forth to pick up goods. Imagine living in the shadow of one of these ports.

Where to go from here: A few important things must happen to lower the environmental impact of cargo ships and ports, including regulating these industries with respect to the fuel they use and how they behave in dock, accelerating the move to electric vehicles, and our own decisions to buy less.

Key Takeaway:

Accelerate our move to electric, be more intentional about travel, purchase less, advocate for transportation industry environmental legislation.

Notes:

-
-
-
-
-
-
-

Reduce your transportation-related carbon footprint.

This shift is about becoming more aware of the impact of our personal travel and purchasing decisions on our carbon footprint.

Step 1: Build your awareness

- Determine your transportation carbon footprint. One good way to do this is by using the carbon footprint calculator at www.carbonfootprint.com or www.coolclimate.berkeley.edu.

Step 2: Take action

Consider electric when making your next car purchase

- If possible, make your next auto purchase an electric car. Electric is the future of automobiles. Volvo and GM are the latest to announce plans to go all-electric by 2025. There are now great choices at all price points, including the secondary resale market. Leaf, Tesla, Volt, i-MiEV, Focus, and Bolt are a few examples, and there are more coming. Electric cars are higher in efficiency than gas-powered vehicles, reduce dependence on fossil fuels, and require less maintenance than most cars. It's time to say goodbye to the combustion engine!

If you are not yet electric, consider the following:

- Go easy on gas and the brakes. Abrupt changes in speed require more gas, so driving with care can help reduce emissions.

- Stop idling, and consider asking your children's schools to implement a no-idling pickup and drop-off policy.

- Regularly service your car. Getting regular tune-ups and oil changes will keep your engine cleaner and emissions lower. A simple tune-up can boost miles per gallon anywhere from 4 to 40 percent. A new air filter can get you up to a 10 percent boost.

- Check your tires. Low tire pressure hurts your fuel economy.

- Use your car's air-conditioning more sparingly. Air-conditioning can increase a vehicle's fuel consumption by 20 percent.

- Don't weigh your car down with unneeded items. The heavier your vehicle is, the less efficient it is. Check if you have items in your trunk that could be removed.

- Car pools are more than just a way to get your kids to and from school—they can be for adults too. Consider carpooling to work, parties, dinners, events. It starts the party earlier!

Whether or not your car is electric, if your job allows it, consider telecommuting for work a day or two a week.

- When possible, consider biking for short-distance trips. Standard or electric—both are great options when considering the planet.

Take public transit

- Let someone else do the driving. Using public transportation reduces overall greenhouse gas emissions and saves an estimated 4.2 billion gallons of gasoline annually in the United States. Enjoy the ride by bringing along something to read or listening to music or a podcast. Apps such as Moovit, Transit, and Citymapper make getting to your destination easier by providing real-time arrival information for nearby public transportation services.

Fly when it matters

- Flying will always be a part of life for many. The opportunity now is to rethink business travel. Are there times when a digital meeting would be just as productive as being there in person? Telecommute is the new cool.

- Speaking of cool—there is now a hipper version of the old Greyhound bus. New bus routes and great service experiences are becoming popular with millennials and GenZ. Megabus and BoltBus are leading the way with affordable tickets, Wi-Fi, comfortable reclining seats, and onboard restrooms. Food and drink can't be far behind.

- Consider traveling by train when it makes sense. With more consumer support, we would likely see greater investment in our rail system. Rail travel is a relatively low-carbon means of travel.

- Consider buying carbon offsets for miles flown.

Buy less stuff made in faraway places

- To be sure, we all buy, and will continue to buy, some products that have been manufactured in overseas markets. The key is to buy less overall and to lessen the number of things we buy from overseas. Check tags and labels to see manufacturing country of origin.

Shop efficiently

- Consolidate your purchases, whether e-shopping or shopping in physical stores. Taking fewer trips, whether it's you or the e-commerce delivery van, cuts down on carbon emissions.

Become an advocate

- Demand that your government representatives and the leaders of all political parties commit to regulating industries that are the largest contributors to transportation-based pollution. The key is to require companies to implement meaningful game plans to effect this transition.

- Advocate for investment in renewable energy as part of a comprehensive move away from fossil fuel–based transportation.

- If you live in the United States (or have family there), consider joining **Mom's Clean Air Force**. This is a community of over a million moms and dads fighting to protect their children from air pollution and the changing climate. They work across the US on national and local policy issues through a network of state-based field teams.

- Check out other groups working on air pollution, including the Coalition for Clean Air in the United States and the Climate and Clean Air Coalition in Canada.

- Download a free air quality app to keep up-to-date on current air pollution levels in your neighborhood.

A note on energy efficiency at home

While we are on the subject of lowering your carbon footprint, consider making your home more energy efficient.

Where we sleep, eat, and live offers a myriad of ways to lower our carbon footprint and save money.

NRDC has long worked to create and champion high-efficiency standards for energy consumption at home. As a result of their work, and that of others in the technology industry, there have been vast improvements in the efficiency of household appliances including air conditioners, thermostats, and lightbulbs.

There is so much money to be saved by creating an energy-efficient home. Visit www.nrdc.org or www.smarterhome.org to learn about all the potential ways to save energy (and money) at home.

Some specific things you can do:

- Seal drafts and insulate adequately.

- Buy low-energy-use bulbs. Turn the lights out whenever you leave a room.

- Pull the plug. Don't leave fully charged devices plugged in to outlets.

- Use power strips for multi-device charging and easy turnoff.

- If possible, purchase a programmable thermostat. It costs $100 or less and can cut energy consumption in your home by 20 percent or more.

- When you are ready, upgrade to energy-efficient appliances. Look for the EnergyStar label.

- Run your dishwasher only when full. If you do this, in addition to saving water, you can avoid emitting 100 pounds of carbon dioxide pollution per year.

- At night or when you're away, lower your thermostat.

- Periodically replace air filters in air conditioners and heaters.

- Close the curtains. Drawn curtains keep the heat and cool in.

- Clean the lint trap in your dryer every time you use it.

- Consider a ceiling fan. These powerhouse workers can make a room feel 10 percent cooler.

- Time to give up on gas-powered leaf blowers. This "convenience" designed to replace manual raking or sweeping is adding more pollution to the air than a car or truck. The gas emitted is harmful to human health and to the person operating the blower. Along with the noise pollution and CO_2 emissions, leaf blowers also lift hazardous substances (dirt, mold, pollen, pesticides) into the air we breathe.

Raise an Environmentalist

Unless someone like you cares a whole awful lot,
nothing is going to get better. It's not.

—Dr. Seuss

One of the most powerful and lasting things you can do as
a parent is to foster an awareness and love of nature in your
children. Raise an environmentalist and you have released into
the world an advocate for balance and harmony.

On that note, it feels like the right time to give a shout-out to all
the parents of the kids, and of course the kids themselves, who
participated in the student marches and walkouts inspired by
world activist Greta Thunberg. An astonishing 4 million people
turned out for the youth-led climate actions in September 2019.
It's hard to believe that Greta was only 15, in ninth grade,
when she began her protest effort. Young people really are
changing the climate movement. So ...

Share the ideas in this book with your kids, and make caring for the environment a part of your family's everyday life. There are so many fun activities to do with children that will strengthen their appreciation for our planet and their role in keeping it clean and healthy. Below are some suggestions to spark your thinking.

Build their love affair with nature

- Do stuff outside even if you have to bundle up. Studies show being outside reduces stress in kids and adults.

- Dig in the dirt and play with worms and other bugs. Let your kids get dirty and muddy, first because it is fun—and then because it introduces good bacteria into their bodies.

- Go bird-watching, explore the outdoors.

- Add birdhouses to your yard. Some birds really like a roof over their head, and that is where you can help out. The simpler the birdhouse, the better. According to Audubon, the best time to put one up is the fall or winter. This way the birds have plenty of time to settle in before breeding. Birdhouses attract birds who will then help out in your garden by eating bugs and the seeds of weeds, and by pollinating.

- If you go to the beach, or to your local park, bring along a bag to pick up plastic trash. Your kids will be amazed at how quickly it fills up. Make it fun by assigning points for commonly found items (5 points for a balloon with string attached, 4 points for a plastic bottle, 3 points for a plastic utensil, 1 point for a bottle top, etc.). Photograph your findings and post them on social media. Challenge your friends. Give the high scorer a special treat.

Garden Together

If you have a backyard or balcony, plant lettuce or carrots, greens or herbs, and let the kids taste the produce they grow themselves. There is nothing more magical than seeing a child's wide-eyed response when pulling a carrot from the ground.

- Go hiking.

- At the right time of year, visit a farm or orchard and show your kids how food grows.

- Frequent your local farmers' markets. (FYI, farmers always appreciate small bills and exact change.)

- Give your child their own little space in the garden or a pot or two to grow and care for their own plants.

- Talk about pollinators such as bees, birds, and butterflies. Add plants and shrubs to your yard that attract them.

Kudos to Parents

It feels like the right time to give a shout-out to the parents who are encouraging their kids to be caring of our planet. You have done a great job raising caring humans who are also environmentalists! And let's start with Greta Thunberg's mom and dad. In 2018, and only in ninth grade, 15-year-old Greta Thunberg walked out of class to express passionate discontent. Her protest began after record-breaking heat waves and wildfires swept through Sweden. Student walk-outs demanding climate action have been growing all across the world ever since. That is, until COVID-19 put a temporary halt to some of the actions. But they will return. Young people are supercharging the climate movement, and not a second too soon. Over 4 million turned out for the youth-led climate marches in September 2019, and several new organizations, led by youth, have taken up the mantle demanding action. Kudos to all you parents!

Useful plants include: aster, bee balm, butterfly bush, calendula, cosmos, daylily, and delphinium. Plant them in clusters so they are easy for the birds and insects to spot!

- Set up a bird feeder together and keep it clean and full.

- Visit national, state, and provincial parks on vacations.

Inspire your kids to be activists

- Join marches, walkouts, and protests for the environment. Make homemade signs together expressing your family's views.

- Bring your kids into conversations about elections and share why you are making the environment a voting issue.

- Discuss issues at dinner. Debate all sides. Remember that many kids are very worried about climate change and its impact on the world they are just beginning to understand. Support them with constructive ideas to mobilize and act. A good antidote to depression is action—making a difference yourself.

- Check out youth-founded and youth-led organizations to share with your kids how much young people can do. Some examples: Zerohour, the Year's Project, the Sunshine Movement, Youth Climate Leaders, Sustainable Youth Canada.

A Butterfly Highway

Get your school engaged with planting milkweed along the monarch butterfly migration route, to counteract the damage being done to the monarch population by pesticides. NRDC is working with students, teachers, and volunteers to create a "butterfly highway" by planting milkweed along 286 miles of road. Monarch Watch is providing milkweed to schools so they can establish a larger network of monarch "way stations."

Teach and inspire

- When you are recycling at home, or doing other things that are good for the environment, involve your kids in the process so they learn too.

- Explain to your kids why you are serving them water from the tap and engage them in filling their water bottles. It's a great teaching moment.

- If you have time, try making Halloween costumes with your kids, rather than buying them. It's about kids learning to work with what you have.

- Inspire your kids with books such as David Suzuki's *There Is a Barnyard in My Kitchen*, David Suzuki and Sarah Ellis's *Salmon Forest*, Greta Thunberg's *No One Is Too Small to Make a Difference*, and *A River Ran Wild* by Lynn

Cherry. Then have a lively discussion. There are more titles, sorted by age, in the Appendix.

- Look into Roots & Shoots, the Jane Goodall Institute's youth-led global community program. It partners with schools, educators, and youth organizations to inspire and educate young people to make a difference on an individual level.

- Start an environmental club at your school. Look into youth groups such as Young Voices for the Planet, Youth Conservation Corps, and Sustainable Youth Canada.

Engage with respected environmental groups

- Search for organizations that are doing great work for the environment and consider making small donations as a family to one or two you most admire. Impact Matters, Charity Navigator, GuideStar, and Founders Pledge will guide you to the nonprofits having a real impact.

- Consider planting a tree or giving a tree as a gift or in someone's honor.

- Learn about groups such as Tree Canada, Tree People, or One Tree Planted, 1t.org, all of which are charitable organizations dedicated to reforestation.

Green your kids' birthday parties

- Set your table with reusable plates, cups, and utensils; avoid plastic straws, paper tablecloths, and single-use plastic utensils — and NO glitter.

- Go paperless with Evite or Paperless Post for invitations.

- Ditch the balloons. These plastic flying machines are responsible for the deaths of countless marine mammals, turtles, and seabirds. Instead, consider fun alternatives such as kites, bunting, pinwheels, ribbon dancers, or felt pompoms, all of which can be used many times for different celebrations.

- Create green loot bags with plastic-free items such as crayons, books, and stationery in reusable cloth sacks.

- When your kids are attending birthday parties, look for gifts with minimal or no plastic.

- If you are bringing a gift to a child's birthday party, consider wrapping it in something reusable or recycled, such as newspaper or previously used wrap.

- Encourage your favorite birthday gift brands, like Lego, to accelerate their timeline for using recycled materials.

A Note to New Moms & Dads

By Harvey Karp, M.D.
Pediatrician; Author, *The Happiest Baby on the Block*;
Inventor, SNOO

"Waaaaaah! Waaaaaah!" Who knew that a sharp scream that comes the second your baby is born would be the sweetest sound ever. And that this moment would be just the first in a series of miraculous moments you will experience as a new parent.

Another miracle. Having a baby instantly transforms your identity. From here on you are first and foremost a parent ... a mom or a dad. You are now a protector, a nurturer. (And, yes, also a diaper changer.)

Now your greatest joy and biggest responsibility is giving your child the very best chance for happiness. Even as you lovingly focus on feeding and soothing your baby, you will start to ponder your next big job—keeping this child healthy and safe.

As you journey through **Imagine It!**, it will become clear that creating a safe home for your child means much more than "child-proofing." It also means protecting against hidden risks like pesticides and pollutants sometimes found in food and water; and hormone-bending phthalates in soft plastic toys.

It is also true that becoming a parent magically bridges the distance between ourselves and the future. It broadens our concerns to what the world will become in 50 and 100 years. It turns enviro-neutral bystanders into fierce warriors for the well-being of the planet. What air will my child breathe? What water will he/she/they drink? Will my child—and others—suffer terrible heat waves, storms, or flooding?

Recent parent warriors have already had impact. Ridding cancerous pesticides from some of our food and dangerous chemicals from hair spray; pulling brain poisoning lead out of house paint and gasoline; stripping toxic chemicals from infant toys and teethers; beginning the push for organic baby food and clothing—with much still to be done.

Your words and actions can stack the deck in favor of your child's health and the health of the planet he/she/they will inherit. No one can do everything, but everyone can do something.

So, start small, but please ... start today!

Teach your kids how to cook!

- Go shopping together for groceries, trying your best to avoid plastic packaging, and then hit the kitchen. Help your children understand how being thoughtful about what we cook and what we eat can be great for both our health and our planet. Cooking is fun to do together and has an added bonus: it encompasses both science and math learning.

Watch nature and wildlife shows and documentaries as a family

- We love *Planet Earth*, *The Nature of Things*, *Here We Are: Notes for Living on Planet Earth*, *Seven Worlds One Planet*, *Blue Planet*, films by BBC Earth, and anything narrated by David Attenborough or on the National Geographic Channel.

Conserve energy as a family

- When leaving the house, remind kids to turn off lights, power down computers, and turn off TVs.

- Encourage them not to linger in front of an open refrigerator or freezer. Explain that this wastes energy.

- Make "turn off the tap" a family motto. Do it when soaping hands, brushing teeth, and doing the dishes.

- Talk to them about taking shorter showers.

- When eating out, put your kids in charge of being the plastic straw police by reminding the server not to give them to you when ordering drinks (once they arrive, it's too late!).

Get off the "upgrade" treadmill

- Enjoy what you already own and teach your kids to resist every shiny new upgrade on their gadgets. Teach them how to navigate the constant bombardment and manipulation of advertising.

- Don't throw things away. Pass them down—clothes, books, toys, shoes. Or pass them along for other kids to use.

- Be a role model. The best way to teach your kids is by being a good role model yourself.

Want to take the next step?

- Sign up and be personally trained in climate science and grassroots organizing by former US vice-president Al Gore. He runs training sessions several times a year all over the world. Join the 20,000 people who have already taken this training and gone on to give presentations at their local library, school, or town hall. Participants' ages range from 12 to 87. Learn more at www.climaterealityproject.org.

Notes:

-
-
-
-
-
-
-
-
-
-
-

"My main recommendations are: Go faster, this is all about pace. Root your efforts in justice, because that's both right and effective. The battle is not to swap out coal for sun; it's to swap out a poisoned and unfair world for one that works for everyone, now and in the future."

—Bill McKibben

Founder, 350.org

CLOSING THOUGHTS

———

Reverend Lennox Yearwood Jr.
President & Founder – Hip Hop Caucus; Environmental Activist

My activism for racial justice and my activism for climate justice are one and the same.

The climate crisis and environmental injustice play out within the same systems of white supremacy and structural racism that are also at the root of police brutality.

Communities who are most impacted by police brutality are the same communities that are the most vulnerable to climate change. People of color have been dying and suffering because of environmental racism and the pollution from dirty fossil fuel infrastructure in our communities at the same time that we have been dying at the hands of racist policing.

Racism is the common denominator.

When Eric Garner was killed by police in New York in 2014, he cried out the same words that George Floyd cried out in Minneapolis: "I can't breathe."

Here's the thing: Eric Garner had asthma. So did his children, including his late granddaughter Erica, who died after suffering an asthma-induced heart attack and a broken heart fighting for justice for her father. The borough Eric lived in received an F for ozone pollution, per the American Lung Association's 2018 report.

You see, there are many ways our communities can't breathe. Sixty-eight percent of Black people live within thirty miles of a coal-fired power plant. Disproportionate pollution in our communities causes higher rates of lung and heart disease, which right now are making us more vulnerable to Coronavirus. Further, according to new research that looked at 32 million births in the United States, African-American mothers and their babies face harm—such as low birth rate, premature births, or stillborns—at a much higher rate due to exposure to high temperatures and air pollution.

Racial justice, health, safety, and the environment are deeply interconnected.

Centuries of systemic racism and oppression have led to unfair and unjust policies in everything from housing and urban development to industry practices—making communities of color more vulnerable to climate impacts. The old saying can be used to explain climate impacts: when white America gets some rain, Black America floods.

Take, for instance, hurricanes. Rising global temperatures from climate change have created warmer oceans and higher sealevels. This has made hurricanes more intense and destructive. Communities of color are in the crosshairs of these supercharged storms and bearing the brunt of them. Look no further than the destruction caused by Hurricanes Katrina, Maria, and Harvey, and Superstorm Sandy. Our communities were left behind.

I encourage you to look at the climate crisis and racism through the same lens, for it truly is the same problem. Seek out people of color, especially young people who are leading in the climate movement, and follow them.

We cannot achieve climate justice without racial justice, and we cannot achieve racial justice without climate justice. The right to breathe clean air, drink clean water, access healthy and safe food, and live in a safe environment is the civil and human rights struggle of this century. We must get it right, for the sake of our children and future generations. And we can get it right, if we fight for justice and our climate at the same time.

A longer version of this essay was first published on www.shondaland.com.

WHAT MAKES LIFE WORTHWHILE?

———

Thomas Homer-Dixon, PhD
Director, Cascade Institute, Royal Roads University

What makes life worthwhile?

We ask ourselves this question sometimes, but usually only when we're experiencing a crisis or a period of extreme change. We might ask it when someone we love is critically ill, or when we've suffered a career setback that has filled us with self-doubt, or when isolation from friends and family confronts us with deep loneliness. Otherwise busyness and buzz—the endless stream of day-to-day tasks we must complete to keep our lives on track, as well as the ceaseless distractions of social media—happily divert us from any question about what matters.

But now an age of crisis is upon us, and everyone around the planet is affected. This crisis may not be obvious in our daily lives, until a massive storm caused by the atmosphere's warming smashes into our cities or until wildfires fill our skies with smoke. Yet even when it isn't obvious, the crisis is still slowly pushing in on us from every side. The natural systems that sustain our health and prosperity—that give us the abundant water we need to drink, the clean air we need to breathe, and the pollinators we need to fertilize our crops—are becoming unstable. And in some cases, they're starting to fail.

"If we do not stop this trend very soon," says the renowned climate scientist Stefan Rahmstorf, "we will not recognize our Earth by the end of this century."

So it's time to step back from our daily busyness and buzz to reflect on—and to start talking among ourselves about—what really makes life worthwhile.

The vision of the "good life" that countless advertising images portray today emphasizes personal physical pleasure: lounging on a tropical beach, living in a luxury high-rise condominium, or driving a fast car along a winding mountain road. This vision of what's worthwhile and the massive material consumption the vision encourages are not only totally at odds with Earth's failing natural systems, they also don't remotely meet our real psychological needs. Once our basic physical requirements for food, shelter, and security are met, consumption of further material stuff is far down just about everyone's good-life list. Give us happy and healthy loved ones, supportive community, a satisfying identity as part of a group, rewarding work, moral purpose, some control over our destiny, and solid reasons for hope, and you'll give most of us nine-tenths of what we really desire in a good life.

The values we need now, the values that will help us define and pursue what makes life worthwhile on a desperately wounded planet—and that will help us heal those wounds—must be profoundly relational. They must start from the recognition that we're all embedded in, and can only thrive within, vigorous networks of life. These are networks of connections not just within our families, communities, and nations, but also spanning global society. Most vitally, they're networks of connections with other living things and with the flows of life-giving elements that sustain us all.

In a world where such interdependence finds new importance, the pursuit of justice and fairness inside and among our societies and in our relationships with nature must take center stage. Human fate isn't divisible anymore; it's not the case that some of us will flourish this century, while others will perish. We'll either all flourish together—all human beings in our incredibly diverse communities and circumstances, and all the living systems that sustain us—or we'll all decline and fail, together.

This wonderful book has given us practical knowledge to help us begin to repair our relations with the people, communities, and nature around us. Its implicit answer to the question—What makes life worthwhile?—is the kind of happiness that comes from working to create a world in which all people and life, together, reach their full potential and flourish in the future. Now, let's make that world real.

DESIGN FOR ALL OF LIFE

———

Bruce Mau

Founder of Bruce Mau Studio and Massive Change Network

For most of the history of Western culture we have been told that we are separate from and above nature. That we own it, that we have dominion over it, that it is limitless and ours to use up as we see fit. Today, science clearly shows that none of that is true. But still this old way of thinking, which puts humans at the center of the universe and against nature, dominates our imagination. What we need is a new mindset—a shift—a new way of seeing who we are and where we are in the universe.

We need to put life, not humans, at the center. When we put life at the center and understand our place in the cosmos alongside and connected with the rest of life, we come to honor and respect life with all other living creatures. We join life. We see ourselves and the way that we live in concert with an awesome symphony of continuity and beauty, ever changing and evolving in a magical exploration of form and possibility. We see our lives and everything that we produce and consume as part of the natural world—not separate from or above nature, but an expression of our natural being.

The moment that we choose to live with intention, to be deliberate of the outcomes of our way of life, we become designers. The way that we live is either random, accidental, and haphazard—or designed. What the authors argue for is a life-centered design mindset. Choosing to design the things that make up our world. Life-centered design means that we understand our lives as a continuous flow of matter and energy in a never-ending cycle. Life-centered design is a Copernican shift in our way of life—a new narrative that breaks from the classical archetype of "man against nature." Life-centered design is a culture of caring. First for ourselves as individual citizens, then for our communities, because we cannot have a thriving individual in a toxic community, and from there we extend our caring to the environment, because we cannot have a thriving community in a toxic ecology.

Let's take this life-centered understanding of our place in the cosmos and experience a new way of being.

FULL SPEED AHEAD

———

Gina McCarthy
White House National Climate Advisor,
Biden Administration
Former President, NRDC
13th Administrator, Environmental Protection

I like to joke that there are only three things you need to know about climate change: Number one, it's real. Number two, *man-made* emissions caused it. And number three, that's why women need to run the world! And while I'm kidding—sort of—there's nothing funny about the fact that climate change is already here. People can increasingly see the impacts of it across our world.

Just look at the wildfires, hurricanes, drought, extreme heat, and more that are hitting close to home for too many. We can see that every single one of us is at risk, and we also know that Black, Brown, Indigenous, and low-income communities are getting hit first and worst. It's just not fair.

Clearly, it's time to act on climate. The good news is, more and more of us are doing just that every day. We are working in our homes, schools, workplaces, communities, and states to accelerate the adoption of climate solutions that save us money, keep our air and water clean, help keep our families healthy and safe, and grow the clean energy jobs of the future. And we are standing together to demand the clean energy future we will be proud to hand to our children.

It is not too late to tackle climate change. In fact, I am more hopeful than ever that clean, efficient energy is winning in the marketplace and the transition away from fossil fuels is accelerating. I see hope in the faces of the thousands of passionate young climate activists around the globe commanding the attention of world leaders. And I have faith in the people like you who are asking what you can do to build a better world.

Together, that's exactly what we are going to do. We're going to do it by becoming advocates for communities on the front lines of the climate crisis. We're going to make the changes we can make in our own lives—and we're going to demand policies from our leaders that leave no one behind.

It's full speed ahead toward a safer, healthier, more just and equitable tomorrow—and we're never looking back.

Draft Advocacy Letter

Example Draft Letter to be sent to a CEO

Your name
email or address

To: David S. Taylor, President and CEO of Procter & Gamble

Subject line: Stop flushing forests down the toilet

Dear Mr. Taylor,

As a consumer concerned about our environment, I was upset to learn that Charmin toilet paper is still being sourced from 100 percent virgin trees, many of them from Canada's beautiful boreal forest.

Not only does the Canadian boreal forest store vast amounts of carbon, it's also home to hundreds of Indigenous communities and to the iconic boreal caribou.

It is unconscionable for majestic old-growth trees to be cut down to make a disposable product that could just as easily be made with recycled fiber.

People look to a brand as venerable as Procter & Gamble to lead—to be an example of innovation toward protecting our planet. You have the power to change this destructive paradigm on a massive scale by reducing the overall use of virgin pulp content in your products.

Until you stop making products that are harmful to our ecosystem, I will be buying my toilet paper and other of your products from a more responsible brand—and doing all I can to encourage others to do the same.

Thank you.

Glossary

B Corps
Certified B Corporations are businesses that commit to consider the impact of decisions on workers, customers, suppliers, the community, and the environment. The Certified B Corporation designation is a legally binding designation that means the company must comply with all environmental safeguards. Examples of Certified B Corps: AllBirds, Stonyfield, Danone Yogurt, Patagonia, Eileen Fisher, Uncommon Goods, Bombas, Frank & Oak, BeautyCounter.

Behavioral contagion,
sometimes called **social contagion**
A type of social influence; the tendency for a person to copy the behavior of others whom they have been exposed to and admire.

BPA (Bisphenol A)
An industrial chemical used to make certain plastics and resins that has been linked to cancer, obesity, and other health issues. It can be found in the lining of canned foods and drinks, plastic water bottles, and cash register receipts.

Carbon footprint
The amount of carbon dioxide emitted through the burning of fossil fuels as a result of the activities of a person or business.

Circular economy
An economic system aimed at eliminating waste and continually reusing resources.

Climate change
A change in climate patterns attributed largely to increased levels of carbon dioxide in the atmosphere due to the burning of fossil fuels. This term was coined during the George W. Bush administration to describe our climate crisis because it sounded less threatening than "global warming." It was widely adopted thereafter.

Climate crisis
What we're in right now. An umbrella term for global warming, the impacts of climate change, and their consequences.

Compost
Decayed organic material used as a plant fertilizer. Compost is rich in nutrients.

Cradle to cradle design
The term *cradle to cradle* was developed by Professor Michael Braungart and architect William McDonough and has since become a respected sustainability concept. *Cradle to cradle* is a designation that indicates there is no waste. The goal of this designation is to inspire a new industrial revolution that ensures production and manufacturing have a positive impact on society, the economy, and our planet.

Deforestation (clear-cutting)

The removal of a forest or stand of trees from land that is then converted to a non-forest use.

Eco-anxiety

Eco-anxiety or climate anxiety was described by the American Psychological Association in 2017 as "a chronic fear of environmental doom."

Environmentalist

A person who acts with intention toward the environment and is concerned with and/or advocates for the protection of the environment.

Factory farm

A system of rearing livestock (poultry, pigs, cattle) indoors and in confined conditions.

Forest Stewardship Council (FSC)

Pioneers of forest certification, this council was set up by a voluntary group of businesses in response to the lack of an agreement to halt deforestation at the 1992 Earth Summit in Rio. The FSC promotes responsible, respectful management of the world's forests.

Fossil fuel

A fuel (such as coal, oil, or natural gas) that was formed from the fossilized remains of prehistoric plant and animal life and which emits high levels of carbon dioxide when extracted and burned to provide energy.

FSC Certification

This certification ensures that products come from responsibly managed forests that provide environmental, social, and economic benefits. The FSC logo is a world standard and is applied to products made through sustainable practices.

Global warming

The ongoing rise of the average temperature of the Earth's atmosphere, generally attributed to the greenhouse effect caused by increased levels of carbon dioxide and other pollutants.

Green living

The adoption of a sustainable lifestyle that is designed to protect the planet and its diverse inhabitants.

Green marketing

Communicating to a customer that a product or service is beneficial for both the environment and the user.

Greenhouse gas

A gas that absorbs radiation, traps heat in the atmosphere, and contributes to the greenhouse effect. According to climate scientists, our human activities are the primary cause of the increase in greenhouse gases over the last 150 years.

Greenwashing

The act of misleading customers and potential customers into believing that a product or service is environmentally friendly and has positive health consequences when this is not true.

Herbicide

A substance that is toxic to plants, used to destroy unwanted vegetation. Also known as weed killer.

Humane

Produced in a manner that causes the least amount of harm to people and animals.

Methane

A heat-trapping greenhouse gas that is roughly 25 times more potent than carbon dioxide.

Monoculture

The cultivation of a single crop in a given area.

Natural

A vague term used on a wide array of products that does not require any real certification and is widely misused to give a perception that the product is healthy.

Neonicotinoids, also known as neonics

A toxic class of neuroactive insecticide chemically similar to nicotine.

Off-gassing

Term for a product slowly releasing a noxious gas. It can sometimes be identified by "new carpet" or "new car" smell, but it can also be odorless.

Organic

Used to describe a food or other material grown without the use of chemical fertilizers, pesticides, or other artificial products. Food given the USDA organic label, or in Canada, the Canada Organic label, has met strict production and certification requirements.

Pesticide

A substance used to destroy insects.

Petrochemicals

Chemical products obtained by refining petroleum.

Regenerative farming

A system of farming principles and practices that increases biodiversity, enriches soils, improves watersheds, and enhances ecosystems.

SFI Certification

Certification from the Sustainable Forestry Initiative (SFI) ensures that products come from responsibly managed forests. The SFI logo is world standard and is applied to products made through sustainable practices.

Sustainable

A word used to describe a non-exploitive, self-renewing approach to the Earth's resources.

Synthetic chemicals

Chemicals made by humans using methods different from those used by nature; these chemical structures may or may not be found in nature.

Upcycle

To reuse discarded items in a way that gives them new life, form, use, and value.

Viscose

A type of rayon fiber that is made from natural sources such as wood and agricultural products.

Young Activists to Follow on Social Media

Jamie Margolin
Founder and coexcutive director of Zero Hour, a youth movement fighting climate change.
Twitter @jamie_margolin
Instagram @jamie_s_margolin

Leah Thomas
Supporter of intersectional environmentalism and founder of Green Girl Leah.
Twitter @leahtommi
Instagram @greengirlleah

Wanjiku "Wawa" Gatheru
An environmental justice scholar and outspoken supporter of empowering BIPOC communities; founder of Black Girl Environmentalist.
Twitter @wawagatheru
Instagram @wawa_gatheru

Xiye Bastida
A Mexican-Chilean climate justice activist and founder of the Re-Earth Initiative.
Twitter @xiyebastida
Instagram @xiyebeara

Dr Ayana Johnson
Marine biologist, climate advocate, co-editor of All We Can Save, *cocreator/cohost @how2saveaplanet*
Twitter @ayanaeliza

Mikaela Loach
Climate justice and antiracism activist focused on sustainability with inclusivity.
Twitter @mikaelaloach
Instagram @mikaelaloach

Alexandria Villaseñor
Latina climate activist and organizer, founder of @earth_uprising
Twitter @alexandriaV2005
Instagram @alexandriav2005

Lucy Biggers
Sustainability producer, host of One Small Step *by NowThis News.*
Twitter @LLBiggers

Lauren Singer
Environmentalist and blogger on zero waste.
Twitter @trashis4tossers

Kate Nelson
Plastic-free advocate and one of Australia's leading environmental advocates.
Instagram @plasticfreemermaid

Vic Barrett
Fellow with the Alliance for Climate Education, spoke at COP21, part of the group of young people who sued the government for inaction on climate.
Twitter @vict_barrett
*Instagram @vicbarrett_*

Isra Hirisi
Co-founder and co-executive of the Youth Climate Strike; also a part of MN Can't Wait, a youth coalition in Minnesota.
Twitter @israhirsi
Instagram @israhirsi

Environmental Groups

Below is a partial list of organizations and agencies working on behalf of the environment.

Resource Note: You can research any organization you are considering working with by running the name through Charity Navigator or Charity Intelligence Canada. These groups evaluate nonprofits.

350.org
A climate activist group with chapters in over 180 countries.

1t.org
An organization committed to planting 1 trillion trees to end deforestation.

5 Gyres Institute
An organization that works on the global crisis of plastic pollution.

Alliance for Climate Education
Educates students in the US through their website, community action, and storytelling.

American Forests
A conservation group working in the US and Canada to advance the conservation of forests.

AZUL
An organization working with Latinx to conserve coasts and oceans.

CanopyPlanet.org
A Canadian group that works with the forest industry's biggest customers and their suppliers to develop business solutions that protect endangered forests.

Center for Rural Enterprise and Environmental Justice
This group seeks to address the root causes of poverty through sustainable solutions.

Climate Justice Alliance
This group challenges the extractive economy that is harming people and ecosystems.

Climate Reality Project
Started by former VP Al Gore, this group works on education and advocacy related to climate change.

Conservation International
Protects lands and coastal areas in partnership with business and governments.

Cool Effect
A nonprofit whose mission is to reduce carbon emissions.

David Suzuki Foundation
A science-based organization working to protect the natural environment and help create a sustainable world.

Defenders of Wildlife
Washington-based advocates for wildlife on Capitol Hill.

Earth Guardians
This group empowers young people to bring solutions to the world's most pressing environmental issues.

Earth Island Institute
This group supports activism through fiscal sponsorships. Founded by environmentalist David Brower.

Earthjustice
Environmental law organization.

Eden Projects
On a mission to employ impoverished peoples through reforestation.

Environmental Defense Fund
An environmental advocacy group.

**Environmental Justice
Health Alliance**
This organization works on chemical policy reform, supporting the movement toward safe chemicals and clean energy that leaves no community or worker behind. EJHA includes an alliance of many environmental justice and grassroots groups.

Environmental Working Group
An American advocacy group that specializes in research and consumer guidance in the areas of food, toxic chemicals in personal care and cleaning products, and drinking water pollutants.

Fibershed
A group working on regenerative farming and educating the public on textile systems.

Fridays For Future
An international youth movement providing the tools to organize school strikes to influence policy makers on Climate Change.

Friends of the Earth
An advocacy group focused on justice and the planet.

Green 2.0
An advocacy group working to increase racial diversity among environmental groups.

Green Latinos
Latino leaders focused on environmental and conservation issues affecting the Latino community in the US.

Greenpeace
Founded in 1970, this nonprofit has a presence in over 40 countries and is known for its Detox Movement against consumption as well as its fleet of boats deployed to physically block oil tankers from leaving port.

Hip Hop Caucus

A US national nonprofit that aims to promote political activism on social issues and the environment for young voters using hip hop and music.

Indigenous Environmental Network

An alliance of grassroots Indigenous peoples whose mission is to protect the sacredness of Mother Earth.

Jane Goodall Institute

This institute is dedicated to protecting chimpanzees and other great ape populations at risk from increasing habitat destruction and illegal trafficking. Jane Goodall's program "Roots & Shoots" motivates kids to become a global movement of youth, using their voices and actions to become more involved in sustainable decisions and develop a respect for the natural world.

Kiss the Ground

This organization focuses on healthy soil to reverse climate change.

Lonely Whale Foundation

An incubator for ideas that drive positive change for our oceans.

Mission Blue

This agency works on promoting a global network of marine-protected areas. Founded by famed oceanographer Dr. Sylvia Earle.

Moms Clean Air Force

Over a million moms and dads united against air pollution.

NAACP

This program focuses on environmental injustice and how climate change has a disproportionate impact on communities of color.

National Audubon Society

An American nonprofit conservation organization working to protect birds and wild places.

National Black Environmental Justice Network

An environmental justice organization dedicated to improving the lives of Black people.

National Wildlife Federation

This federation works to protect wildlife.

Nature Conservancy

A conservancy working to protect the lands and waters on which all life depends.

NRDC (Natural Resources Defense Council)

A world-leading international environmental advocacy group that combines the law, science, lobbying, and legislation to ensure the rights of all people to a sustainable environment.

Oceana
An international group focused on protecting the world's oceans.

Ocean Clean Up
Based in the Netherlands, this group develops technology to extract plastic pollution from the oceans.

One Percent for the Planet
Started by Patagonia's Yvon Chouinard, this certification requires members to commit 1 percent of their profits toward environmental action.

PEW Charitable Trust
Founded in 1948, this trust's conservation efforts are focused on preserving wild places and rivers and increasing understanding of biodiversity and ocean ecology.

Power Shift Network
A North American nonprofit made up of youth-led environmental justice groups working together for the climate movement.

Project Drawdown
A nonprofit of scholars, scientists, and advocates focused on drawing down global warming pollution.

Rainforest Alliance
This alliance works at the intersection of business, agriculture, and forests to protect critical ecosystems around the world and make responsible business "the new

normal" to further a better future for people and the planet.

Regeneration International
This group works to promote and accelerate the transition to regenerative farming and land management.

Sea Shepherd Conservation Society
An international nonprofit and marine wildlife conservation organization.

SeaLegacy
Started by photographer Paul Nicklen, this is a collective of photographers, filmmakers, and storytellers focused on the oceans.

Sierra Club
One of the first environmental groups in the US, founded in 1892 by John Muir, this grassroots organization is dedicated to enjoying, exploring, and protecting the Earth for everyone.

Sunrise Movement
A youth-led political movement advocating action on climate change.

Sustainable Harvest International
Works to improve well-being through sustainable farming.

Texas Environmental Justice Advocacy Services
This organization promotes environmental protection of communities through education, policy, awareness, and legal action.

Tree People
A Los Angeles–based organization that educates youth to stand up for the environment and plants trees.

Union of Concerned Scientists
Science advocacy organization made up of both scientists and private citizens using science to effect positive change for a healthy world.

Urban Ocean Lab
A think tank for the future of coastal cities.

Water.org
A global organization working to bring water and sanitation to the world.

WE ACT for Environmental Justice
This group empowers and organizes low-income people of color to build healthy communities.

WeForest
An NGO working on replanting to fight global warming.

Wildlife Conservation Society
Dedicated to saving wildlife and wild places worldwide.

World Wildlife Fund (WWF)
An organization committed to conserving nature and reducing threats to the diversity of life on Earth.

Yale Climate Connections Research
A communications center focused on climate.

Youth Climate Leaders
A youth-led global network connecting young people around the world to catalyze climate action and careers.

Websites Worth Visiting

Shift 1: Plastic
www.conservation.org
www.davidsuzuki.org
www.eartheasy.com/articles/plastics-by-the-numbers/
www.nationalgeographic.org
www.nrdc.org
www.oceancleanup.org
www.plasticoceans.org
www.plasticpolutioncoalition.org
www.sirwaggingtons.com
www.thisisplastics.com
www.wbur.org

Shift 2: Food
www.fao.org
www.seafoodwatch.org
www.foodsustainability.eiu.com
www.nrdc.org
www.ota.com
www.wbur.org/hereandnow/2019/09/20/how-to-recycle-plastic

On food, Environmental Working Group's Food Scores guide gives their take on nutrients, contaminants, additives, and processing for tens of thousands of food products. This is in addition to the Dirty Dozen guide mentioned in Shift 2. Both the Food Scores information and the Skin Deep info on cosmetics are included in the Healthy Living App for iOS and Android.

Shift 3: Clothing
www.goodonyou.org
www.sustainyourstyle.org
www.fashionrevolution.org
www.tulerie.com
www.threadup.com
www.poshmark.com
www.realreal.com

Shift 4: Chemicals
www.ucsf.edu
www.ewg.org
www.chemicalsinourlife.echa.europa.eu
www.davidsuzuki.org
www.nrdc.org
www.safermade.net
www.homefree.healthybuilding.net

Healthy Living: Home Guide goes through every room in the house with tips for identifying problems and options for reducing chemical exposures.

Advocacy
www.act.nrdc.org/letter/monarchs-180412
www.act.nrdc.org/letter/epa-bee-170829

Shift 5: Paper
www.canopyplanet.org
www.foreststewardshipcouncil.org
www.nrdc.org
www.theworldcounts.com

Shift 6: Water
www.water.org

For water, see EWG's Tap Water Database. Enter your zip code and find out about what's in your water, EWG's take on the health implications, and filters that can reduce or eliminate specific contaminants found.

Shift 7: Transportation
www.carbonfootprint.com
www.carbonzero.com
www.coolclimate.berkeley.edu
www.energysage.com
www.yaleclimateconnections.org
www.nrdc.org
www.smarterhome.org

Raising an Environmentalist
www.lcv.org
www.climaterealityproject.org

ADDITIONAL WEBSITES

Environmental Health Justice Alliance
www.ej4all.org

Environmental Paper Network
www.environmentalpaper.org/hereandnow/2019.how-to-recycle-plastic

www.atmosfair.com
www.charitynavigator.org
www.earthisland.org
www.grist.com
www.onetree.org
www.organicauthority.com
www.pacinst.org/worlds-water-challenges-2017/
www.scorecard.lcv.org
www.thegoodtrade.com
www.treehugger.com
www.ucsusa.org/sites/default/files/legacy/assets/documents/global_warming/palm-oil-and-global-warming.pdf
www.wellnessmama.com
www.worldcentric.com

Recommended TV, Films & Documentaries

There are hundreds of fabulous nature shows on National Geographic, the BBC, Disney, and other channels and streamers. This list just features some of our favorites.

Acid Test: The Global Challenge of Ocean Acidification
NRDC's award-winning documentary.

An Inconvenient Truth
A 2006 ground-breaking documentary about former US vice-president Al Gore's efforts to teach people about global warming.

An Inconvenient Sequel
Part two of *An Inconvenient Truth*, 10 years later.

A Plastic Ocean
A 2016 documentary about plastic pollution in the world's oceans.

Ashes and Snow
The 2005 documentary by Canadian artist Gregory Colbert exploring the connections between people and animals.

Avatar
A blockbuster science fiction film by director James Cameron about the planet's poisonous environment.

Before the Flood
Actor Leonardo DiCaprio discusses climate change with experts.

Biggest Little Farm
An award-winning documentary about a young couple who adopt a dog and end up on an epic adventure creating a regenerative farm.

Blackfish
2013 doc about an orca at SeaWorld and the controversy over killer whales.

Blue Planet
Acclaimed British TV series narrated by Sir David Attenborough about the world's oceans.

Blue Vinyl
This documentary uncovers the health and environmental risks associated with the widely used plastic polyvinyl chloride, also known as PVC.

Chasing Coral
Director Jeff Orlowski's follow-up to *Chasing Ice*, focusing on our vanishing coral reefs.

Chasing Ice
2012 doc about the efforts of photographer James Balog to capture the planet's melting glaciers.

Cowspiracy
A doc about the true impacts of industrial animal agriculture.

DamNation
A 2014 advocacy doc about the changing attitudes in the US concerning the large system of dams.

Dark Skies
This story dramatizes Robert Bilott's case against the chemical manufacturing corporation DuPont after they contaminated a town with unregulated chemicals.

Erin Brockovich
A classic tale of an everyday woman who goes up against the energy corporation Pacific Gas and Electric.

Food, Inc.
Filmmaker Robert Kenner examines how mammoth corporations have taken over all aspects of the food chain. Blockbuster hit that led the way for many other films examining our food systems.

Frozen Planet
From the Planet Earth team, this seven-part series looks at the Earth's polar regions.

Gasland
A Josh Fox–directed film that looks at natural gas drilling and fracking.

GMO OMG
A father examines the relationship between genetically modified food and his three young children.

Interstellar
In Earth's future, a global crop blight and second dust bowl are slowly rendering the planet uninhabitable.

Jane
A biographical doc film, directed by Brett Morgen, about anthropologist Jane Goodall.

Kiss the Ground
Science experts unpack the ways in which the Earth's soil may be the key to combating climate change and healing the planet.

Last Animals
Follows conservationists, scientists, and activists battling poachers and criminal networks to protect elephants.

Last Call at the Oasis
A look at the role of water and potential water shortages ahead. Includes the real Erin Brockovich as an advocate.

March of the Penguins
A 2005 French feature-length nature documentary that broke all kinds of records. Worth revisiting!

Nature (PBS)

Wildlife television program produced by award-winning PBS. Over 38 seasons and hundreds of episodes covering animals and ecosystems.

No Impact Man

Colin Beavan gives up his modern lifestyle to go completely green in a drastic effort to lessen his environmental impact.

Planet Earth

A multi-part series of awe-inspiring natural wonders from the sea to the deserts to polar ice caps.

Poisoning Paradise

From Pierce and Keely Brosnan, this is a doc about pesticide use in Hawaii.

Racing Extinction

About humankind's role in the potential loss of at least half of the world's species. Directed by Louie Psihoyos, who also did *The Cove.*

RiverBlue

A documentary that follows conservationist Mark Angelo around the world as he uncovers the dirty secrets behind how our clothes are made.

Sea of Shadows

A National Geographic film about the effort to rescue the Earth's smallest whale—the vaquita—from extinction and a crime syndicate.

Silkwood

An oldie-but-goodie drama starring Meryl Streep, about a union activist and nuclear whistle-blower.

Sonic Sea

A NRDC film shedding light on the hazards of ocean noise pollution. A real eye-opener!

Stories from the Gulf

Narrated by Robert Redford, a powerful 22-minute doc about the impact on Gulf residents of the largest oil spill in American history.

Syriana

A drama by Stephen Gaghan about the Middle Eastern oil industry.

Tapped

A doc that examines the financial and ecological impacts of the bottled water industry, including the toxic by-products of manufacturing plastic water bottles. Directed by Stephanie Soechtig and Jason Lindsey.

The China Syndrome

The classic 1979 drama/thriller about a whistle-blower at a nuclear power plant.

The Cove

A riveting doc following activist Ric O'Barry as he tries to shed light on the Japanese practice of capturing dolphins.

The Day After Tomorrow

A 2004 "what if" tale about a climatologist whose warnings about environmental disasters are ignored.

The Devil We Know

Based on a true story, and directed by Stephanie Soechtig, this is about how the making of Teflon ended up polluting a community in West Virginia.

The Human Element

This film directed by James Balog captures the ways environmental change is affecting the lives of everyday people.

The Island President

A documentary about the president of the Maldives and his efforts to save his country from the impacts of the climate crisis.

The Ivory Game

A film examining the ivory trade.

The Lorax

The story of a 12-year-old boy who lives in a place devoid of nature, based on the book by Dr. Seuss.

The Nature of Things

Debuted in 1960! This Canadian television series, hosted by famed environmentalist David Suzuki, deals with all aspects of our impact on nature.

The Pollinators

A doc about a journey around the United States following migratory beekeepers and their truckloads of honeybees as they pollinate the flowers that become the fruits, nuts, and vegetables that get eaten.

The Salt of the Earth

A documentary about Brazilian nature photographer Sebastião Salgado.

The Story of Stuff

A series of short films about the life cycle of material goods. Annie Leonard unravels things in a unique and engaging way. Watch these with your kids.

Vanishing of the Bees

This film follows commercial beekeepers David Hackenberg and Dave Mendes as they strive to keep their bees healthy.

Virunga

A gripping, Academy Award–winning documentary about the conservation work of four park rangers within Congo's Virunga National Park—home to the world's last mountain gorillas.

Wasted: The Story of Food Waste

The filmmakers explore the reasons we waste so much food.

Winged Migration

This beautiful epic portrait examines the winter bird migration. Filmed on all seven continents over four years.

Years of Living Dangerously

A TV series examining the climate crisis.

KIDS' MOVIES & DOCUMENTARIES

A Beautiful Planet
Stunning look at Earth—and man's sobering impact on it.

FernGully: The Last Rainforest
An animated eco doc about a fairy who lives in FernGully, a rain forest in Australia, and has never seen a human before.

Happy Feet
Into the world of the Emperor Penguins, who find their soul mates through song, a penguin is born who cannot sing.

Here We Are: Notes on Living on Planet Earth
Narrated by Meryl Streep, this is a beautifully animated version of Oliver Jeffers's best-selling book by the same name.

I Am Greta
Documentary follows teenage climate activist Greta Thunberg on her international crusade to get people to listen to scientists about the world's environmental problems.

Ice Age: The Meltdown
A 2006 American computer-animated adventure comedy film.

Our Planet
A series focusing on the impacts of climate change on all living creatures, starring Sir David Attenborough.

Police Patrol
Computer-animated film with strong pro-environment message.

To the Arctic
Educational documentary explores life in the frozen wild.

WALL-E
A clever animated tale from Disney about a lonely robot who spends his days picking up trash.

Recommended Books

THE ENVIRONMENT

*A Sand County Almanac:
With Essays on Conservation
from Round River*
Aldo Leopold

*All We Can Save: Truth,
Courage, and Solutions for
the Climate*
Ayana Elizabeth Johnson,
Katharine K. Wilkinson

*An Inconvenient Sequel:
Truth To Power*
Al Gore

*An Inconvenient Truth:
The Planetary Emergency
of Global Warming and
What We Can Do about It*
Al Gore

Animal, Vegetable, Miracle
Barbara Kingsolver

*Cradle to Cradle: Remaking
the Way We Make Things*
William McDonough

*Commanding Hope:
The Power We Have to
Renew a World in Peril*
Thomas Homer-Dixon

*Desert Solitaire:
A Season in the Wilderness*
Edward Abbey

*Don't Even Think about It:
Why Our Brains Are Wired
to Ignore Climate Change*
George Marshall

*Drawdown: The Most
Comprehensive Plan
Ever Proposed*
Paul Hawken

*Earth in the Balance: Forging
a New Common Purpose*
Al Gore

Falter
Bill McKibben

Flight Behaviour
Barbara Kingsolver

*Half-Earth:
Our Planet's Fight For Life*
E. O. Wilson

*How to Avoid a
Climate Disaster*
Bill Gates

*Inconspicuous Consumption:
The Environmental Impact
You Don't Know You Have*
Tatiana Schlossberg

*Keep Calm And
Protect The Planet*
Greta Thunberg

*No One Is Too Small to
Make a Difference*
Greta Thunberg

*Overdressed: The Shockingly
High Cost of Cheap Fashion*
Elizabeth L. Cline

*Rising: Dispatches from
the New American Shore*
Elizabeth Rush

*Silent Spring:
The Classic That Launched
the Environmental Movement*
Rachel Carson

*Six Degrees: Our Future
on a Hotter Planet*
Mark Lynas

Storming the Wall
Todd Miller

The Age of Miracles
Karen Thomas Walker

The Conscious Closet
Elizabeth Cline

*The Death and Life of
Great American Cities*
Jane Jacobs

*The End of Ice:
Bearing Witness and
Finding Meaning in the
Path of Climate Disruption*
Dahr Jamail

The End of Nature
Bill McKibben

The Future Earth: A Radical Vision for What's Possible in the Age of Warming
Eric Holthaus

The Golden Spruce
John Vaillant

The Great Derangement: Climate Change and the Unthinkable
Amitav Ghosh

The Overstory
Richard Powers

The Sixth Extinction: An Unnatural History
Elizabeth Kolbert

The Story of More: How We Got to Climate Change and Where to Go from Here
Hope Jahren

The Tiger
John Vaillant

The Uninhabitable Earth
David Wallace Wells

The Water Will Come: Rising Seas, Sinking Cities, and the Remaking of the Civilized World
Jeff Goodell

The World We Create: A Message of Hope for a Planet in Peril
Frances Beinecke

This Changes Everything
Naomi Klein

We Are the Weather: Saving the Planet Begins at Breakfast
Jonathan Safran Foer

What We're Fighting for Now Is Each Other: Dispatches from the Front Lines of Climate Justice
Wen Stephenson

ENVIRONMENTAL JUSTICE

A Terrible Thing to Waste: Environmental Racism and Its Assault on the American Mind
Harriet A. Washington

All Our Relations: Indigenous Struggle for Land and Life
Winona LaDuke

As Long as Grass Grows: The Indigenous Fight for Environmental Justice, from Colonization to Standing Rock
Dina Gilio-Whitaker

Black Faces, White Spaces
Carolyn Finney

Black Food Geographies
Ashanté M. Reese

Braiding Sweetgrass: Indigenous Wisdom, Scientific Knowledge and the Teachings of Plants
Robin Wall Kimmerer

Cadillac Desert: The American West and Its Disappearing Water, Revised Edition
Marc Reisner

Cultivating Food Justice: Race, Class, and Sustainability
Alison Hope Alkon

Clean and White: A History of Environmental Racism in the United States
Carl Zimring

Earth Democracy: Justice, Sustainability, and Peace
Vandana Shiva

Farming While Black: Soul Fire Farm's Practical Guide to Liberation on the Land
Leah Penniman

Freedom Farmers: Agricultural Resistance and the Black Freedom Movement
Monica M. White

From the Ground Up: Environmental Racism and the Rise of the Environmental Justice Movement
Luke W. Cole

On Fire: The Burning Case for a Green New Deal
Naomi Klein

Our History Is the Future
Nick Estes

Parable of the Sower
Octavia Spencer

Rooted in the Earth
Dianne D. Glave

Soil Not Oil
Vandana Shiva

Tales of Two Planets
John Freeman

The Death and Life
of the Great Lakes
Dan Egan

The Hungry Tide
Amitav Ghosh

The Mushroom at
the End of the World
Anna Lowenhaupt Tsing

The Shock Doctrine
Naomi Klein

The Yellow House
Sarah Broom

There's Something in the
Water
Ingrid R. G. Waldron

Waste: One Woman's Fight
Against America's Dirty Secret
Catherine Flowers

Winning the New Green Deal
Varshini Prakash

Youth to Power: Your Voice
and How to Use It
Jamie Margolin

COOKBOOKS

Bad Manners:
The Official Cookbook
Bad Manners Staff

Cool Beans
Joe Yonan

Eat for the Planet
Gene Stone

Eat for the Planet: Saving the
World One Bite at a Time
Nil Zacharias

Eating Animals
Jonathan Saffron Foer

Five Ingredient Vegan
Katy Beskow

Food52 Vegan
Gena Hamshaw

Forest Feast Mediterranean
Erin Gleeson

Forks over Knives—
The Cookbook
Del Sroufe

Forks over Knives: Flavor!
Darshana Thacker

Greenfeast: Autumn, Winter
Nigel Slater

Greenfeast: Spring, Summer
Nigel Slater

How to Cook
Everything Vegetarian
Mark Bittman

I Can Cook Vegan
Isa Chandra Moskowitz

Love Is Served
Seizan Dreux Ellis,
Café Gratitude

Love Real Food
Kathryne Taylor

Made with Love
Kelly Childs,
Erinn Weatherbie

Minimalist Baker's
Everyday Cooking
Minimalist Baker Staff,
Dana Shultz

Mostly Plants
Tracy Pollan, Dana Pollan,
Lori Pollan, Corky Pollan

Oh She Glows Every Day
Angela Liddon

On Vegetables
Jeremy Fox, Noah Galuten

Plenty More
Yotam Ottolenghi

The Art of Simple Food:
Notes, Lessons, and Recipes
from a Delicious Revolution
Alice Waters

The Buddhist Chef
Jean-Philippe Cyr

The First Mess Cookbook
Laura Wright

The Greek Vegetarian Cookbook
Heather Thomas

The Homemade Vegan Pantry
Miyoko Schinner

The Modern Cook's Year
Anna Jones

The New Vegetarian Cooking for Everyone
Deborah Madison

The Oh She Glows Cookbook
Angela Liddon

Ultimate Veg
Jamie Oliver

Vegan Everything
Nadine Horn, Jörg Mayer

Vegan Reset
Kim-Julie Hansen

Veganomicon, 10th Anniversary Edition
Isa Chandra Moskowitz, Terry Hope Romero

KIDS AGES 3–5

10 Things I Can Do to Help My World
Melanie Walsh

Anywhere Farm
Phyllis Root

Clifford's Spring Clean-Up
Norman Bridwell

Compost Stew: An A to Z Recipe for the Earth
Mary Mckenna Siddals

Here We Are: Notes for Living on Planet Earth—A Special Edition
Oliver Jeffers

I Am Jane Goodall
Brad Meltzer

I Can Save the Earth!: One Little Monster Learns to Reduce, Reuse, and Recycle
Alison Inches

Miss Rumphius
Barbara Cooney

The Earth Book
Todd Parr

Winston of Churchill
Jean Davies Okimoto

KIDS AGES 6–9

Ada's Violin: The Story of the Recycled Orchestra of Paraguay
Susan Hood

Can You Hear the Trees Talking? Discovering the Hidden Life of the Forest
Peter Wohlleben

Curious George Plants a Tree
H. A. Rey

Don't Let Them Disappear
Chelsea Clinton

Energy Island: How One Community Harnessed the Wind and Changed
Allan Drummond

Follow the Moon Home: A Tale of One Idea, Twenty Kids, and a Hundred Sea Turtles
Philippe Cousteau, Deborah Hopkinson

Give Bees a Chance
Bethany Barton

If Sharks Disappeared
Lily Williams

Kate, Who Tamed the Wind
Liz Garton Scanlon

Life in the Ocean: The Story of Oceanographer Sylvia Earle
Claire A. Nivola

Manfish: A Story of Jacques Cousteau
Jennifer Berne

Merhorses and Bubbles
Asia Citro

Michael Recycle
Ellie Bethel

Michael Recycle Meets Litterbug Doug
Ellie Bethel

Miss Fox's Class Goes Green
Eileen Spinelli

Nature's Day:
Out and About: Spotting,
Making and Collecting
Kay Maguire,
Danielle Kroll

Oil Spill!
Melvin Berger

One Plastic Bag: Isatou
Ceesay and the Recycling
Women of the Gambia
Miranda Paul

Our House Is on Fire:
Greta Thunberg's
Call to Save the Planet
Jeanette Winter

Rachel: The Story
of Rachel Carson
Amy Ehrlich

Recycle! A Handbook for Kids
Gail Gibbons

Shark Lady: The True Story of
How Eugenie Clark Became the
Ocean's Most Fearless Scientist
Jess Keating

The Adventures of a Plastic
Bottle: A Story about Recycling
Alison Inches

The Boy Who Harnessed the
Wind: Young Readers Edition
William Kamkwamba,
Bryan Mealer

The Curious Nature Guide:
Explore the Natural Wonders
All Around You
Clare Walker Leslie

The Lorax
Dr. Seuss

The Nature Connection: An
Outdoor Workbook for Kids,
Families, and Classrooms
Clare Walker Leslie

The Ocean Story
John Seven

The Tree Lady: The True
Story of How One Tree-Loving
Woman Changed a City Forever
H. Joseph Hopkins

The Wonders of Nature
Ben Hoare

This Is the Earth
Diane Z. Shore,
Jessica Alexander

Trash Talk: Moving Toward
a Zero-Waste World
Michelle Mulder

What a Waste:
Trash, Recycling, and
Protecting Our Planet
Jess French

What Is Climate Change?
Gail Herman

What's So Bad about
Gasoline? Fossil Fuels
and What They Do
Anne Rockwell

Where Does the Garbage Go?
Paul Showers

Why Are the Ice Caps
Melting? The Dangers
of Global Warming
Anne Rockwell

Why Should I Protect Nature?
Jen Green

Why Should I Recycle?
Jen Green

Why Should I Save Energy?
Jen Green

Why Should I Save Water?
Jen Green

Wolf Island
Celia Godkin

POETRY

An American Sunrise: Poems
Joy Harjo

Black Nature: Four Centuries
of African American Nature
Poetry
Camille T. Dungy

Devotions
Mary Oliver

From Unincorporated Territory
Craig Santos Perez

The World-Ending Fire:
The Essential Wendell Berry
Wendell Berry

Some of Our Favorite Products

FOR THE KITCHEN:
COFFEE FILTERS

1. DripKit
   - *Committed to creating a 100% biodegradable product and paying farmers fair wages in the process.*

COMPOST

2. Bamboozle Compost Bin
   - *Made of biodegradable, dishwasher-safe, and durable bamboo fiber.*

3. Public Goods Compostable Waste Bag
   - *BPI-certified compostable plant plastic bags.*

4. Full Circle Fresh Air Kitchen Compost Collector
   - *Permits oxygen to flow through organic kitchen waste, allowing aerobic breakdown. Food decomposes more slowly and stays drier during the composting process, resulting in less mess, less odor, and no flies.*

5. Living Composter
   - *Designed to compost on your countertop, this odorless, biomorphic composter turns food scraps into fertilizer. Worms and microorganisms inside the composter actively break down food waste on your countertop.*

6. STACK 4L Food Waste Compost Caddy
   - *Features built-in odor filter compartments and biodegradable bag inner liner.*

7. Seed & Sprout Compost Bin
   - *Built-in charcoal filter under the lid to neutralize odors.*

DISH DRYING RACKS

8. Yamazaki Dish Rack
   - *Japanese storage brand Yamazaki.*

9. Rig Tig Dish Drying Rack
   - *Danish brand Rig Tig is known for kitchen essentials and classic serveware (under parent brand Stelton).*

10. Five Two Over-the-Sink Drying Rack
    - *This drying rack rolls out, fits over sinks of all sizes, and stows away in seconds. Silicone-coated stainless steel holds up under hefty pots and supports delicate glassware alike.*

ECO DINNERWARE & COOKWARE

11. Ekobo Bamboo Dinnerware
    - *Made from bamboo, a highly renewable natural resource, and a 100% food-grade melamine binder; plus, they're BPA, PVC, and phthalates free.*
    - *Dinnerware, kitchenware, and other food storage essentials.*

12. Bamboozle Bamboo Dinnerware
    - *Made from dishwasher-safe bamboo fiber, these dinnerware sets are sustainable, chemical-free alternatives to melamine.*
    - *100% biodegradable*

13. Fable Bamboo Dinnerware
   • *Crafted from bamboo fiber and non-GMO cornstarch.*

14. Caraway Home Cookware
   • *Teflon and chemical free ceramic pots & pans.*

15. GreenPan Cookware
   • *An incredible alternative to traditional nonstick pans, GreenPan has a special ceramic coating that ensures a nontoxic finish no matter how high you turn up the heat.*

16. Material Kitchen reBoards
   • *Made from recycled plastic and renewable sugarcane, these kitchen cutting boards require zero virgin plastic and are one step closer to a sustainable kitchen.*

17. Scanpan CS+ Skillets
   • *Teflon and chemical free, Scanpan CS+ is completely PFOA and PFOS free from the start of the manufacturing process to the finished product.*

18. Lodge Cast Iron Chef Collection Skillet
   • *Seasoned with 100% natural vegetable oil for an easy-release finish.*
   • *Use in the oven, on the stove, on the grill, or over a fire.*

KITCHEN UTILITY

19. Seed & Sprout Silicone Baking Mats
   • *Fit perfectly on oven trays for baking and can be used over and over again (alternative to parchment paper).*
   • *Dishwasher & oven safe*

20. Silpat™ Silicone Cookie Baking Mat
   • *Silpat™ Cookie Mat could be used in the oven, microwave, and freezer. The Cookie Mat can be reused thousands of times.*

21. If You Care Parchment Paper
   • *Made from 100% unbleached paper, and is biodegradable, compostable, and landfill safe.*
   • *Manufactured materials are all made from renewable resources and the packaging materials are made from recycled paper.*

22. JK Adams Lazy Susan
   • *Walnut lazy Susan—something you will want to keep for years to come. For use in fridge or on kitchen table.*

LUNCH, MARKET, & PRODUCE BAGS

23. Dans Le Sac
   • *Canadian*
   • *Boutique retailer and wholesaler with a custom-designed line of sustainable products, set to reduce waste and chemical footprint—natural/organic cotton and linen.*
   • *Authors of* Minimal

24. SoYoung
   • *Canadian brand of elevated lunch bags on a mission to make packing your lunch sustainable, stylish, and self-empowering.*

25. Baggu
    - *Designed to minimize waste, leveraging sustainable materials (ripstop nylon).*
    - *Long partnership with overseas manufacturer committed to ethical and environmentally responsible practices.*

26. Ever Eco
    - *Australian eco-conscious brand focusing on the elimination of household plastics.*

27. OUI Lunch Totes
    - *Designed to work with OUI's storage containers for healthy meals on the go*

28. OUI Waxed Canvas Lunch Bag
    - *Waxed cotton canvas for reusable lunch.*

29. Seed & Sprout Bulk Food Bags
    - *Organic cotton muslin*
    - *Perfect for fine/loose dry goods like nuts, grains, cereals, seeds, powders.*

30. Seed & Sprout Mesh Produce Bags
    - *Pure GOTS-certified organic cotton mesh bags.*
    - *Super-lightweight*
    - *Machine washable*

31. OUI Produce Shopping Set
    - *100% cotton, zero-waste alternative to plastic grocery store produce bags. Sold in a set of 3 for easy produce shopping.*

32. Seed & Sprout Market Tote
    - *100% GOTS-certified organic cotton string/canvas.*
    - *Made for bringing home the groceries.*

33. Seed & Sprout Mini Pocket Tote
    - *Made from sturdy GOTS-certified organic canvas.*

34. Seed & Sprout Pocket Tote
    - *6 large internal pockets keep things organized, balance weights, and stop jars and veg from banging up against each other.*
    - *Carries an average of 3 standard bag loads.*

PAPER TOWELS

35. Marley's Monsters Un-Paper Towels
    - *Organic cotton paper towel alternatives (reusable and machine washable).*

36. Cheeks Ahoy
    - *Organic cotton paper towel alternatives (reusable and machine washable).*

25

26

27

28

29

30

31

32

33

34

35

36

37. Indigo Linen Napkins
    • *100% linen that gets softer with each use.*
    • *Machine washable*

38. Ten & Co Swedish Sponge Cloths
    • *Reusable, compostable printed dishcloths that can wring and dry like a normal paper towel.*

39. KLIIN Reusable Towel Roll
    • *Compostable, machine-washable kitchen cloth that replaces need for disposable paper towels.*

40. Skoy Earth-Friendly Cloths
    • *Skoy is a 100% biodegradable, reusable, and compostable cleaning cloth. Made using all-natural materials (cotton and wood pulp cellulose). Skoy can absorb 15x its own weight and each one can outlast 15 rolls of paper towels.*

41. If You Care Natural Sponge Cloths
    • *Compostable, cellulose-based paper towel alternative.*

42. Washable Bamboo Fleece Duster
    • *Alternative to paper towels or disposable dusting cloths, made from multiple layers of organic cotton and viscose bamboo.*
    • *Duster tendrils will curl after washing to make the collection of dust more effective.*

UTENSILS

43. Porter x W&P Utensils
    • *Balancing design and sustainability with a product assortment that offers a full range of reusables to replace wasteful single-use plastics while eating and drinking on the go.*
    • *Limited edition books accompany the assortment.*

44. Go Sip x Final Touch
    • *Canadian*
    • *Portable kit of reusable straws in both glass and stainless steel.*
    • *Multicomponent for adapting to a variety of different drinks while on the go, as well as for easy cleaning.*

45. Ever Eco
    • *Australian eco-conscious brand focusing on the elimination of household plastics.*

FOR FOOD & DRINK STORAGE:

CLEAR FOOD STORAGE

46. Kilner Glass Food Storage Containers
    • *Borosilicate glass storage containers with glass lids.*

47. Zwilling J.A. Henckels Borosilicate Glass Storage Container (Set of 2)
    • *Made from thermal shock-resistant borosilicate glass.*

48. Pyrex Ultimate 10-Piece Variety Set
    • *Borosilicate and silicone storage containers for use in the fridge or on the go.*

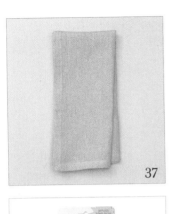

37

38

39

40

41

42

43

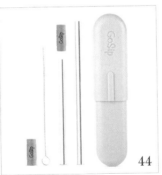

44

45

46

47

48

49. Maison Plus Borosilicate
Storage Containers
- *Sets of borosilicate glass storage containers for leftovers and food storage in the fridge or to take to the office.*

50. Mepal Modula Stackable
Storage Containers
- *Made in the Netherlands, Mepal is known for functional kitchen prep tools and storage items.*

51. Berghoff Glass Storage Set
- *Set of 3 borosilicate glass and silicone storage containers.*
- *Countertop (for bulk shopping) and fridge storage sizes available.*

52. Airtight Kitchen Canisters
- *The original Airscape® coffee and food storage canister with patented lid actively removes and locks out air to preserve and protect freshness and flavor.*

53. Airscape® Lite Storage Containers
- *The Airscape® Lite features the same patented food-preserving technology in a stackable, durable, BPA-free, phthalate-free plastic container body. For use inside the fridge or on the countertop.*

54. Hawkins New York Glass Simple
Storage Containers
- *Glass countertop storage with oak or walnut lids.*

FOOD STORAGE CONTAINERS

55. Seed & Sprout Eco Stow Sets
- *Glass containers are microwave, freezer, oven, and dishwasher safe.*
- *Sustainable bamboo lid*

56. OUI Stainless Steel Lunch
Boxes & Thermoses
- *Reusable stainless steel storage containers for portable lunches.*

57. OUI Portable Food Jars
- *Reusable food storage containers for portable lunches.*

58. Mepal Lunchbox Take A Break Midi
- *Danish-inspired design with products that aim to make healthy eating on the go fun, fashionable, and waste free.*

59. Porter x W&P
- *Balancing design and sustainability with a product assortment that offers a full range of reusables to replace wasteful single-use plastics while eating and drinking on the go.*
- *Limited edition books accompany the assortment.*

60. Dalcini
- *Stainless is an award-winning company dedicated to healthy, sustainable housewares without the use of plastic or hormone-disrupting chemicals.*
- *Wide variety of products that range from food storage to travel bottles & hydration, and utensils.*

49

50

51

52

53

54

55

56

salad
protein
vegetables
dressing

57

58

59

60

FOOD SAVERS

61. Stasher
    - *Reusable, nontoxic silicone bags*
    - *Wide variety of bags that can be used for food preservation, cooking (sous vide), and even everyday storage.*
    - *A 1% for the Planet Company*

62. Ever Eco
    - *Australian eco-conscious brand focusing on the elimination of household plastics.*

63. Abeego
    - *Canadian*
    - *Beeswax wrap designed to keep food safe and preserved after first use.*
    - *Made with natural beeswax*
    - *Biodegradable and compostable*

64. Goldilocks
    - *Canadian*
    - *Beeswax wrap designed to keep food safe and preserved after first use.*
    - *Made with natural beeswax*
    - *Biodegradable and compostable*

65. Seed & Sprout Reusable Stretch Lids
    - *Made from food-safe, sand-derived silicone*
    - *Heat-safe, dishwasher-safe, microwave-safe food covers.*

66. Seed & Sprout Food Huggers
    - *Made of food-safe silicone*
    - *Usable on cut fruits or veggies or open cans, jars, & bottles.*

67. OUI Cotton Muslin Bowl Covers
    - *Made from 100% cotton and designed to keep food fresh in your fridge without using plastic food storage wrap.*

68. Seed & Sprout Silicone Food Pouches
    - *BPA free, nontoxic*
    - *Made of sand-derived silicone (no plastic)*
    - *Dishwasher, microwave, freezer safe*

69. Charles Viancin Food Covers
    - *Reusable silicone bowl covers as a swap for plastic wrap.*
    - *Their designs come in shapes inspired by nature, including poppies and lily pads.*

70. Seed & Sprout Food Savers
    - *Reusable silicone bowl covers*
    - *Packaging is made from either recycled paper or compostable cornstarch "plastic."*
    - *A brand with a mission to "unplastic the planet."*

WATER BOTTLES & TRAVEL MUGS

71. S'well
    - *Stainless steel insulated water bottles and travel mugs.*
    - *First fashion hydration brand*
    - *Eliminated their packaging in 2019 in favor of compostable brands for product information.*
    - *A 1% for the Planet Company*

72. Stojo
    - *Reusable, nontoxic silicone travel mugs and water bottles, with a patented design that focuses on durability and transport.*
    - *A 1% for the Planet Company*

61

62

63

64

65

66

67

68

69

70

71

72

73. Keep Cup
   - *Reusable glass (tempered soda) and cork travel mugs.*
   - *Offers an exchange and replacement service in order to reduce discarding of cups over their lifetime.*

74. JOCO
   - *Durable and long-lasting glass travel mugs with downcycled silicone bands and lids.*
   - *Biodegradable packaging and shipping cartons.*

75. Kinto
   - *Japanese-inspired design*
   - *Reusable powder-coated stainless steel water bottles and infusion tumblers.*

76. Stelton
   - *Danish-inspired design*
   - *Stainless steel with plastic (BPA and phthalate free)*

77. SodaStream
   - *Saves on plastic bottles with its reusable and refillable bottle.*

78. Aarke Sparkling Water Maker
   - *BPA-free PET water bottles can replace thousands of single-use plastic bottles.*

FOR CLEANING:

DISHWASHING SOAPS/ KITCHEN SOAPS

79. No Tox Life Dishwashing Block
   - *Vegan dish soap block—suds with H_2O as you would a bar of hand soap.*

80. The Unscented Co. Refillable Soap
   - *Fragrance, dye, and paraben free. Refillable glass soap container with 100% recyclable refill containers.*

81. Nellie's Dish Powder
   - *Water-free dish soap. Refillable.*
   - *A few dashes of powder and scrub your dishes.*
   - *Biodegradable, septic safe, and phosphate free. Above all, this powder is a plant-based formula and kind to the environment.*

82. ETEE Dish Soap Concentrate
   - *Natural dish soap concentrates. Mix with water in bottle and use as normal dish soap.*
   - *Zero waste with biodegradable packaging*

83. ETEE Plastic-Free Dish Soap Bars
   - *100% natural dish soap bar—alternative to liquid dishwashing soaps. Use with scour pad and cellulose wipes to clean dishes and countertops.*

84. Public Goods Castile Soap
   - *100% pure castile soap with all USDA-certified organic, vegetable-based ingredients.*

 73

 74

 75

 76

 77

 78

 79

 80

 81

 82

 83

 84

85. Dropps Dishwasher Detergent Pods
   - *Free of artificial colorants, dyes, and synthetic fragrances.*
   - *Subscription-based service with 100% recyclable or biodegradable packaging.*

86. Seed & Sprout Dish Bar
   - *100% palm oil and plastic free*
   - *Synthetic fragrance free*

PLASTIC-FREE SPONGES & CLEANING SUPPLIES

87. Public Goods Walnut Scour Pad
   - *Walnut-based scrubbing abrasive and all-natural vegetable cellulose.*
   - *100% natural and plastic free.*

88. Full Circle Walnut Scrubbing Sponges
   - *Biodegradable walnut- & cellulose-based sponges. Plastic free.*

89. Sayula Agave Dish Scrubber
   - *This scrubber is handmade from the leaves of the "maguey" agave.*
   - *100% natural fiber. Compostable.*

90. ETEE Loofie Scrubber
   - *Biodegradable scrubber—made from fibrous loofah plant and the spongy cellulose-cotton cellulose dishcloth. They're even sewn together using cotton thread (rather than the all too commonly used polyester thread), which makes for reusable & biodegradable dish cleaning with absolutely no plastic.*

91. Redecker Dish Brush
   - *Natural, reusable alternative to plastic sponges.*
   - *Heritage German brand Burstenhaus Redecker has been making brushes since 1935.*

92. Redecker Pot Brush
   - *Alternative to plastic sponges*
   - *Heritage German brand Burstenhaus Redecker has been making brushes since 1935.*

93. Andrée Jardin Dustpan
   - *Wood and metal dustpan—alternative to disposable plastic cleaning tools*

94. Redecker Copper Cloth
   - *Alternative to disposable plastic sponge scour pads*
   - *Heritage German brand Burstenhaus Redecker has been making brushes since 1935.*

SURFACE CLEANERS

95. Blueland Surface Cleaning Set
   - *Direct-to-consumer tablet-form eco cleaners*

96. Nellie's One Bottle
   - *100% recyclable, reusable spray bottle with glass concentrate cleaners.*
   - *Biodegradable and contains no harsh chemicals, phosphates, or strong perfumes.*

 85

 86

 87

 88

 89

 90

 91

 92

 93

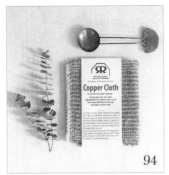 94

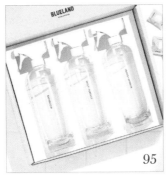 95

 96

97. Public Goods Bathroom & Glass Cleaner Concentrates
   - *Zero waste cleaning agent concentrates— mix with H_2O in your own spray bottle.*
   - *Powered by coconut-derived actives that work hard to clean your bathroom safely and naturally.*

98. Cleanyst At-Home Zero Waste Cleaning Maker
   - *Create home and body care products at home using naturally derived ingredients and tap water—all at the press of a button! Perfectly mixed products and an 80% reduction in plastic waste.*

99. Everspring Cleaning Products
   - *Targets full line of eco-cleaning agents with 100% recyclable packaging.*

100. Cleanpath Refillable Surface Cleaners
   - *Zero waste, eco-cleaning agent concentrates with refillable bottles.*

101. Truman's Zero Waste Cleaning Kit
   - *Refillable, nontoxic cleaning concentrates*

102. Meliora Eco All-Purpose Home Cleaning Spray Set
   - *Plastic-free and nontoxic set uses natural ingredients like organic coconut oil.*
   - *Meliora is a member of 1% for the Planet, and pledges to donate at least 2% of all sales toward nonprofits like the Women's Voices for the Earth.*

103. Mrs. Meyer's Cleaning Products
   - *Cruelty-free formula*
   - *Made with essential oils and other thoughtfully chosen ingredients.*

   - *Recyclable packaging (less pumps & caps)*

104. Seventh Generation Disinfecting Cleaners, Wipes, and Sprays
   - *Made with plant-based cleaning ingredients and packaged with postconsumer recycled plastic whenever possible.*
   - *Seventh Generation is on a mission to transform the world into a healthy, sustainable, & equitable place for the next seven generations.*

105. Method All-Purpose Cleaner
   - *Nontoxic with naturally derived, biodegradable ingredients.*

FOR LAUNDRY:

LAUNDRY DETERGENTS & SOFTENERS

106. Pokoloko Dryer Balls
   - *Improves aeration of laundry, allowing for reduced dryer cycle times.*
   - *Added movement softens laundry during drying and eliminates need for dryer sheets.*

107. Moss Creek Wool Works Wool Dryer Balls
   - *Handmade in Canada*
   - *Reduces drying time, saves electricity, and preserves the life span of your clothing.*

108. Ecoegg Dryer Egg
   - *The innovative Dryer Eggs will cut your drying time, save you money, and soften and fragrance your clothes too.*
   - *The Dryer Eggs contain hypoallergenic, dermatologically tested essential oil fragrance sticks to scent and dry in one product.*

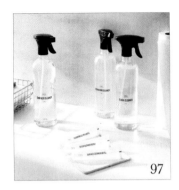

97

98

99

100

101

102

103

104

105

106

107

108

109. TruEarth Laundry Detergent Sheets
    - *Soap strips you tear and throw into laundry.*
    - *Recyclable packaging and reduces need for H_2O-based detergents in plastic bottles.*

110. Unscented Co. Refillable Laundry
    - *Chemical & eco-friendly detergent*
    - *Refillable recycled plastic dispenser Refill packaging is 100% recyclable/ biodegradable.*

111. Public Goods Laundry Detergent
    - *Chemical-free, all-natural, plant-based laundry detergent pods in biodegradable packaging.*

112. Truman's "Get a Load of This" Detergent Pods
    - *Nontoxic laundry detergent pods with 100% recyclable packaging.*

113. The Simply Co Laundry Detergent
    - *100% biodegradable, made from all-natural ingredients that you can actually pronounce; your ingredient list can be found on your recycled and plastic-free packaging.*

114. Soapworks Liquid Laundry Soap
    - *Detergent-free, biodegradable, fragrance-free laundry soap concentrate.*

115. Eco Max Hypoallergenic Laundry Wash
    - *An all-natural, plant-based laundry wash in a hypoallergenic formula for sensitive individuals.*

116. PurEcosheet Reusable Dryer Sheets
    - *Reusable product has all the advantages of a traditional dryer sheet, without all the chemicals.*

117. Soapworks Pure Laundry Soap Powder
    - *Natural, biodegradable, powder-based fabric softening soap that eliminates need for additional chemical softeners or sheets.*

118. Eco Nuts Organic Laundry Detergent
    - *A sustainable laundry experience that's nuts (literally!). Eco Nuts Soap Nuts are actually dried berries from trees in the Himalayas that, when agitated in water, release a natural cleansing agent called saponin—which also acts as a fabric softener.*

119. Dropps Laundry Detergent Pods
    - *Nontoxic laundry detergent pods with 100% compostable or recyclable packaging.*

LAUNDRY RACKS

120. Burstenhaus Redecker Clothespins
    - *In most parts of the world people air-dry laundry, and are not reliant on energy-sucking tumble dryers.*
    - *A set of wood clothespins for air-drying*
    - *Burstenhaus Redecker is a heritage German brush-making company since 1935.*

109

110

111

112

113

114

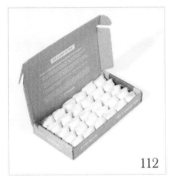

115

116

117

118

119

120

121. Yamazaki Laundry Racks
    - *Japanese brand Yamazaki is known for home organization.*

122. French Steel Clothespins (Set of 24)
    - *We love a classic wooden clothespin, but those metal springs somehow always manage to sneak their way out of their grooves, never to return.*
    - *Made of durable stainless steel and are perfect for hanging laundry.*

FOR BODY:
BATH & BODY

123. Well Kept
    - *Razor is made of solid brass and designed to last a lifetime.*
    - *Razor and blades are plastic free.*
    - *Blades, razor, and packaging are recyclable.*

124. Saalt
    - *Reusable medical-grade silicone menstrual cups.*
    - *B Corp certified*

125. The Honey Pot Company Tampons
    - *Certified organic cotton*
    - *Free from pesticides, chlorine, dioxins, or synthetic materials.*
    - *100% recyclable packaging*

126. Freon Collective
    - *Reusable cotton facecloths and makeup wipes.*

127. Unwrapped Life
    - *Concentrated formulas of soap, condition, and body wash, which reduce the need for plastic packaging and waste.*
    - *Clean ingredient base*

128. Nala
    - *Made in British Columbia, Canada*
    - *All-natural deodorant*
    - *Free from harsh chemicals, aluminum, phthalate, parabens, petroleum, carcinogens.*

129. Hi Bar
    - *Salon-quality plastic-free hair care brand*
    - *No soap, sulfates, parabens, phthalates, or silicones.*
    - *Packaging is completely recyclable and compostable.*

130. Public Goods Shampoo Bar
    - *Created from sustainably sourced organic palm and palm kernel oils, organic olive and coconut oils, organic lavender essential oil blend including rosemary extract and aloe vera.*

131. Fur
    - *All-natural clean-ingredient products that hydrate skin, soften hair, and eradicate ingrown hairs from head to toe.*
    - *Dermatologically and gynecologically tested.*

132. Public Goods Hand Soap
    - *Carefully considered high quality, natural and healthy ingredients.*
    - *Cruelty free & Vegan-Friendly*

121

122

123

124

125

126

127

128

129

130

131

132

133. Dr. Bronner's Liquid Soap
    - *Contains fair trade & organic ingredients*

134. Aesop Déodorant
    - *All Aesop products are vegan and are not tested on animals.*
    - *The bottle is made from a minimum of 97% postconsumer recycled PET.*

135. MALIN+GOETZ
    Eucalyptus Deodorant
    - *Infused with natural eucalyptus and citronellyl to help neutralize odor.*
    - *Formulated without aluminum, alcohol, or parabens.*

GREEN BEAUTY

136. Botanica
    - *Environmentally Friendly Recycled Glass Packaging*
    - *Naturally derived active ingredients*
    - *Vegan & Cruelty Free*

137. Palermo
    - *Truly natural skin care products made by hand in small batches and packaged in Brooklyn, NY.*
    - *Made with natural, quality ingredients and organic and wildly harvested where possible.*

138. Deew
    - *Vancouver-based cannabis products made with clean ingredients.*
    - *Vegan and Cruelty Free*
    - *Ethically Sourced*

139. Province Apothecary
    - *Province Apothecary sources the highest-quality organic ingredients from each Canadian province, and hand-blends in small batches.*

140. Kaia Naturals
    - *100% Cruelty-Free and Nontoxic Beauty Essentials for busy and active lifestyles.*

141. Beautycounter Lipstick
    - *Over 80% of the ingredients in their products are natural or plant-derived.*
    - *Uses a paper lipstick tube made with FSC-certified paper.*

142. Josie Maran Argan Black Oil Mascara
    - *Paraben, sulfate, gluten, phthalate, formaldehyde free*
    - *Synthetic fragrance free*
    - *Cruelty free*

HAND SANITIZER

143. Rocky Mountain Soap Co.
    - *10 OR LESS ingredient strategy; natural origins (i.e., from the earth).*
    - *Does not allow for the use of any ingredient that may be harmful to, or cause the destruction of, any animal habitats, species, or the environment.*

144. By Humankind Hand Sanitizer
    - *Refill bottle is made of aluminum.*
    - *100% carbon neutral*

133

134

135

136

137

138

139

140

141

142

143

144

ORAL CARE

145. Tom's of Maine Natural Toothpaste
    - *Only uses ingredients that meet the brand's Stewardship standards for natural, sustainable, and responsible products.*
    - *The toothpaste tube is recyclable – first-of-its-kind in recycling technology.*

146. Davids
    - *Recycled metal tubes and biodegradable packaging.*
    - *Naturally sourced and derived ingredients: no sodium, lauryl sulfate, or fluoride.*
    - *98% US Origin ingredient list (i.e., locally sourced).*

147. Georganics Toothpaste Tablets
    - *Compostable packaging*
    - *Fluoride, glycerin, and SLS free*
    - *Vegan and cruelty free*

148. Naked Brush
    - *100% biodegradable bamboo toothbrushes for adults & kids.*

149. Coco Floss
    - *Cruelty and toxin free, including parabens, SLS, and PFAS, vegan.*
    - *Leaping Bunny certified, the gold standard in cruelty-free certification for non-animal-tested products.*
    - *Floss refills are in compostable packaging.*
    - *Biodegradable and scented with natural ingredients.*

SUNSCREENS

150. Rocky Mountain Soap Co.
    - *10 OR LESS ingredient strategy; natural origins (i.e., from the earth).*

151. Coola
    - *Every COOLA formula is crafted with at least 70% certified organic ingredients.*

152. Salt + Stone
    - *Ingredients are grown and produced in ethical and sustainable ways.*
    - *Packaging is recyclable and made from postconsumer recycled materials.*
    - *Products are manufactured by renewable solar and hydroelectric energy.*

FASHION

153. Genusee Sunglasses
    - *Ethically made from 15 single-use water bottles.*

154. Allbirds Shoes
    - *Certified B Corp*
    - *Uses materials sourced from nature, like wool from merino sheep and sugarcane.*
    - *Recycled shoe packaging, using 90% postconsumer recycled cardboard.*

155. TOMS Shoes
    - *Certified B Corp*
    - *Supports organizations and causes that improve lives.*
    - *TOMS' earthwise™ products must contain earth-friendly materials in at least one of the main components.*

EXERCISE

156. Wilson Triniti Tennis Balls
    - *100% recyclable packaging*
    - *New plastomer materials maintain liveliness 4x longer.*

145

146

147

148

149

150

151

152

153

154

155

156

Photo Credits

p. 18: Laurie David

p. 20: Jochen Tack / ImageBROKER via Alamy Stock Photo

p. 29: Romeo Gacad / AFP via Getty Images

p. 37: Tim Gainey / Alamy Stock Photo

p. 38: Jim West / Alamy Stock Photo

p. 47: Oksana Bratanova / Alamy Stock Photo

p. 49: Apricot Lane Farms

p. 57: Martin Skultety / Image Professionals GmbH via Alamy Stock Photo

p. 58: Marina Drasnin

p. 60: Konstantin Trubavin / Westend61 GmbH via Alamy Stock Photo

p. 65: Viktor Fischer / Alamy Stock Photo

p. 66: Vladimir Sotnichenko / Alamy Stock Photo

p. 69: Carolyn Jenkins / Alamy Stock Photo

p. 77: Dave Donaldson / Alamy Stock Photo

p. 78: Radius Images / Design Pics via Alamy Stock Photo

p. 79: LightField Studios Inc. / Alamy Stock Photo

p. 82: Peter Bennett / Citizen of the Planet via Alamy Stock Photo

p. 85: Cavan Images / Alamy Stock Photo

p. 86: kkong / Alamy Stock Photo

p. 93: dpa picture alliance / Alamy Stock Photo

p. 94: Natali Alba / Alamy Stock Photo

p. 97: Techa Tungateja / Alamy Stock Photo

p. 101 (top): StockPhotosArt – Objects / Alamy Stock Photo

p. 101 (bottom): Cseh Ioan / Alamy Stock Photo

p. 111: Arto Hakola / Alamy Stock Photo

p. 116: Bobby Bruderle

p. 121: Joshua Windsor / Alamy Stock Photo

p. 124: Gary Crabbe / Enlightened Images via Alamy Stock Photo

p. 131: Matthias Webersberger / CHROMORANGE via Alamy Stock Photo

p. 133: Bet_Noire / iStock by Getty Images

p. 140: Malkin Photography / Alamy Stock Photo

p. 154: Veronica Thompson / Paul Thompson Images via Alamy Stock Photo

p. 158: Canetti / Alamy Stock Photo

p. 165: Rasa Arlauskienė / Alamy Stock Photo

p. 170: Sarah Silbiger / Stringer via Getty Images

p. 173: Laurie David

p. 174: Andrew Benton / Alamy Stock Photo

p. 176: Laurie David

p. 177: Jim West / Alamy Live News via Alamy Stock Photo

p. 181: Olivia Lance

p. 182: Christopher Casler / Alamy Stock Photo

SPECIAL THANKS

———

We want to extend special thanks to the following people who have contributed so much and in different ways to helping bring this book to life:

To Gina McCarthy, former President of NRDC, for her leadership, constant guidance, and inspiration in all ways; and to her incredible staff of experts for their always gracious responses to our endless questions, including the wonderful Sarah Engler (who deserves double thanks!), Darby Hoover, Mae Wu, Jennifer Bernstein, Michelle Egan, Ella Tabasky, Daniel Hinerfeld, Steve Fleischli, Miriam Rotkin-Ellman, Jenny Shalant, Bora Chang, Stephanie Valeria, Jenny Powers, Christina Choi, Ann Lien, Elizabeth Bland, Erika Preuss, Kristen Walsh, and Susan Casey-Lefkowitz.

To Ken Cook and his passionate and deeply knowledgeable staff at the Environmental Working Group for their input and guidance.

To Thomas Homer-Dixon, Reese Halter, Dr. Harvey Karp, Bruce Mau, and Reverend Yearwood for their generous essays.

To Bruce Mau, Nathan Williams, Breanne Woods, and Alison Lee for their beautiful book design, and to Judith McKay for overseeing the production of the book with such care, Tracy Kyncl for organizing the image licensing, and to Navraj Sagoo for keeping track of every page and every change through so many iterations.

To Nina Montee, Cami Gordon, Romy David, Monina Von Opel, Amanda Gauthier, Angela Kohler, Chelsea Cox, Heather Babby, Ellen Babby, and Stephanie Soechtig, who read various versions and gave us great notes.

Finally, to our dear friend Louise Dennys, who made us believe we had a book in us and indulged us with her expert guidance every step along the way.

LD: With deep gratitude and very special thanks to my environmental mentors, including John Adams, Alan Horn, Frances Beinecke, and Vice President Al Gore. And to my husband, Robert Thorpe—my best eco partner.

HMR: To David Suzuki for a lifetime of inspiration and Edward Burtynsky for further opening my eyes.

"Choose only one master— nature.

—Rembrandt